What people are saying about

Gifts from the Devastation

For anyone who has struggled, whether with cancer or another trauma, this book is a must read. Celine takes a radically different perspective on dealing with devastation, charting how she believes life happens for us, not to us. In an increasingly hectic world, *Gifts from the Devastation* is a call to try something different. It is a message worth listening to; a message of hope.
Sarah McInerney, RTE Broadcaster and Journalist

This book brings gifts to all of us who need to refresh our lives if we sense we are not living to our full potential. It is also relevant to anyone experiencing a significant life disruption. The writing is clear and the message is simple – Live your own life to the full.
Dilis Clare, Consulting Medical Herbalist & General Practitioner, MBBCh, DRCOG, BSc (Hons) Herbal Medicine

I would highly recommend this book to anyone who is struggling to overcome difficult life circumstances and who wants to learn practical ways of overcoming the inevitable challenges that life can throw at us.
Tony Óg Regan, Holistic Performance Coach and former Galway Hurler

Gifts from the Devastation

What cancer taught me about life

Gifts from the Devastation

What cancer taught me about life

Celine O'Donovan

BOOKS

Winchester, UK
Washington, USA

JOHN HUNT PUBLISHING

First published by O-Books, 2021
O-Books is an imprint of John Hunt Publishing Ltd., 3 East St., Alresford,
Hampshire SO24 9EE, UK
office@jhpbooks.com
www.johnhuntpublishing.com
www.o-books.com

For distributor details and how to order please visit the 'Ordering' section on our website.

ISBN: 978 1 78904 644 1
978 1 78904 645 8 (ebook)
Library of Congress Control Number: 2020947592

A CIP catalogue record for this book is available from the British Library.

Design: Stuart Davies

UK: Printed and bound by CPI Group (UK) Ltd, Croydon, CR0 4YY
Printed in North America by CPI GPS partners

We operate a distinctive and ethical publishing philosophy in
all areas of our business, from our global network of authors to
production and worldwide distribution.

Contents

One day you finally knew what you had to do, and began....

From "The Journey" by Mary Oliver

Preface

It started with a gentle nudge but soon took on a life of its own. Writing about my experience with breast cancer proved very cathartic. I found a way to express myself and process everything that had happened. This book though is not only about this experience. It is also a reflection on my life and the personal challenges I faced long before cancer. It is about the insights and discoveries that I made along the way. It is about finding a new way of living that has brought me great joy. I hope that by sharing my story it will give you a new perspective on any difficulties you may be facing. Once I started writing it evolved organically, as has my life throughout this writing process. As my story illustrates, there are always warning signs in our life, indicators that are guiding us to make change for our highest good. The topics I cover reflect what I needed to learn so that I could live in a healthier way and I know that the lessons will continue as long as my life unfolds. I can see now that every experience was needed to give my life meaning and help me come into my purpose. Breast cancer was the ultimate manifestation of the many times I had disowned and dishonored myself and kept myself small in the world. I needed to heal my life. I realize that we are all meant to shine as the highest version of ourselves. We are unique in what we came here to express and we should never dim that light just to fit in. I don't regret any experience in my life. Each one has made me who I am today. If I have one wish, it is that you may come to recognize your own magnificence and find your unique way of expressing it in the world. That is the greatest gift of all.

May you find the wisdom to listen to your illness,
ask it why it came,
why it chose your friendship,
where it wants to take you,
what it wants you to know,
what quality of space it wants to create in you,
what you need to learn to become more fully yourself, that your
presence may shine in the world.
Extract – A Blessing for a Friend on the Arrival of Illness
by John O'Donohue

Introduction

I can still recall that day so clearly, 11th February 2016:

> *You have breast cancer with lymph node involvement. You will need chemotherapy, surgery, radiotherapy, all in all probably a year out of your life. We need to start treatment soon.*

I remember hearing the consultant's words, but it was like an out of body experience. Everything stopped and some sort of autopilot kicked in. Everything changes in that moment, the moment that we get devastating news. We all have stories of personal devastations. They are a normal part of the human condition that none of us escape. They are major disrupters to our lives so it is only natural that in the midst of our pain we question why. I did.

The Cambridge Dictionary defines disruption as: *the action of preventing something, especially a system, process or event, from continuing as usual or as expected.*

Life as we know it will never be the same. We are forced to dig deep and in the depths we uncover who we truly are. We discover coping mechanisms and a strength we never knew we had. We may shut down for a while. We might get stuck and suffer. We can feel bitter about our misfortunes or we can suppress how we feel and push on through. These are all normal responses. Indeed they are how I coped with life for many years! However, there is a different choice we can make, in the long term a healthier choice – to fully experience, learn, grow and ultimately thrive on this journey called life.

For as long as I can remember I've felt a great hunger to understand the deeper mysteries of life and the purpose of my existence. My darkest times were when I could find none. So when cancer knocked on my door I was ready to focus only on the lessons and gifts of the experience; lessons that I believe are universal in nature. I'm not saying it was easy because it wasn't. There were times I thought I couldn't go on and I was very angry. However, I knew it had happened for a reason. Even in the midst of feeling vulnerable and lost there was no going back to business as usual. I was done with suffering and fighting with life. I just knew that chapter was over. It took time, but eventually I started to see new possibilities and a different way of being in the world. I now feel more alive than I ever have. It really did take cancer to show me that life as I was living it wasn't working for me anymore. In fact it was killing me.

So too with planet earth. 2020 heralded a new era when our world as we knew it was brought to a standstill. We witnessed one of the greatest disruptions to our existence, and although it brought a lot of pain and heartache, it was surely telling us that business could not continue as usual in our global community. Spiritual teacher Ram Dass says of our breakdowns: *The breaking down of systems is a tool for growth.* As we heal I hope we support each other and work together to rebuild. I hope we focus only on the lessons and the gifts. I hope we use them as fuel to live fiercely in the pursuit of a better life for every person and for planet earth. And I hope that my story of transformation plays some small part in this chapter of our awakening.

Part I – Healing

In the first part of the book I document my experience with breast cancer, the warning signs that were there long before I was diagnosed and the healing it ultimately brought about in my life. Once I stopped and was willing to explore a deeper place in myself, a whole new world started to open up. It was an experience that changed everything and I would go through it all again in a heartbeat, knowing what I know now. In fact, if faced with the choice of going back to relive my life a year prior to cancer or the year of cancer, I would choose the latter, strange as that may sound. It has altered me in ways that I cannot fully express, other than to say that it was something I had to experience.

Chapter 1

A New Direction

Tell me, what is it you plan to do with your one wild and precious life?
Mary Oliver

I had been looking for change in my life and I really hoped that 2016 was going to be the year. I was struggling with some of my relationships and I craved a connection with like-minded people. I felt like I had come to the end of the road in my career and I desperately wanted to work in a more holistic field. I longed to be my own boss despite the uncertainty that goes with it. I yearned for freedom, although I didn't really know what that meant. I just knew that there was a higher calling on my life and I had to find it.

Growing up in Galway city on the west coast of Ireland, I had no idea of the twists and turns my life would take before leading me back home to where it all began. Galway is a colorful melting pot of residents and despite growing rapidly since I was a child, it still retains the intimacy of a small and connected community. From born and bred Galwegians, to "blow-ins" and buskers, students and tourists, everyone mingles easily. I love that about the place. I was born in Salthill, a seaside resort at the edge of the city with breathtaking views of the Atlantic Ocean. Growing up as a middle child, with an older sister and younger brother, I was shaped like we all are, by my position in the family. At times I felt overlooked and unsure, at others independent and free. I dreamt of being fearless and adventurous like tomboy George, in the Enid Blyton *Famous Five* books, yet I was sensitive and often felt anxious with no idea why. I was afraid of nothing and everything at the same time. I had so much I wanted to say and yet I was timid and shy. Only now can I see the internal struggles that vied for my attention from an early age. They have been a recurring theme in my life for many years. As is often the case, it took a lengthy absence in my twenties for me to really appreciate home. It definitely made my heart grow even fonder. I feel very fortunate to come from such a vibrant and eclectic place that embraces diversity in all its forms. Just a short drive west, in stark contrast to the bustling city center, is the wild, barren landscape of Connemara. It feels like my own life now echoes these contrasting environments. I love the richness and community of the city, yet I cherish and need my solitude too. Recuperating from cancer treatment in the city of my birth has brought a sense of completion and healing to my life. I have come full circle. When I returned to live in Galway in 2004, I had no idea that it would be the springboard into my new life when the time was right.

It was 1990 when I first left home for the bright lights of Dublin city. I was twenty-two years of age and had just finished university. I was in the privileged position of having two job offers to choose from and I surprised myself by taking the job in Dublin. It was a marketing role with a large bank, and although I was delighted to be one of only two graduates offered a job there that year, I was nervous at the idea of leaving home for a city that was a total stranger to me. I know the move was written in the stars as it proved instrumental in how my life would play out. I met one of my best friends, Rachel, on my first day at work. We were an unlikely pairing on the surface. She was a sophisticated Dubliner who had just returned from a summer working on Nantucket Island, while I was the country cousin who had just arrived in the capital sporting my own knitted creations. I felt like a total fish out of water and her warm welcome put me at ease straight away. She took me under her wing and from that moment on a bond was forged for life. Despite our physical distance, our connection has only deepened with the years. Within two years I had also met my future husband, Brian. We clicked instantly and ended up working side by side for a few years. Fate obviously stepped in as he was just about to hand in his resignation when he got the transfer. I could never have guessed the important role these two people would play in every chapter of my life and I know that will always be the case. As we were some of the first graduates recruited, we got great training on the job and had some amazing experiences. The thirteen years I spent in the bank have stood to me in everything I have done since. A couple of highlights were travelling to India for the production of a TV commercial and getting to see the world premiere of *Riverdance* in 1995. There were so many more. Living in Dublin caused me to grow up in so many ways. I started a new life there. I learnt to stand on my own two feet. I proved that I could fend for myself. I have retained only happy memories of that time, even though it came to an abrupt end in 2002 when my marriage collapsed. As my world fell apart I was left reeling. Struggling to cope I took a career break and found myself teaching English in Greece. There were many ups and downs along the way, but after a year I eventually made my way back to Galway. I still felt rudderless. Every aspect of the life I knew had just disintegrated before my eyes. As I tried to find my footing, I took up a marketing position in the local university in 2005. It was a life-saver. I was by no means over the trauma of my marriage breakup; still it was a fresh start and gave me a focus. I was grateful for that. I loved the job from day one and the opportunities it gave me to travel the world promoting the university. I spent time in India and after a couple of years I moved to a domestic role where I promoted the university in schools around Ireland. I realized how much I enjoyed educating and supporting young people. I thrived in this environment. It was another great job where I developed many new skills. However, after ten years' travelling, I felt worn-out. I just knew that something had to give. It was 2016 and it is there that I start this story.

Although I was desperate for change, I had no idea it was going to be such a life-changing year. Having developed an interest in all things holistic many years before, I was a regular at all types of retreats and workshops. So as a new year dawned, I attended a retreat organized by a very gifted shaman and healer. I loved coming together with groups of like-minded people, reflecting and setting intentions for a new year. I was determined to start 2016 with renewed energy and direction. It was during a private healing session over the weekend that I got a very clear impression that my life was going to alter dramatically and very soon. Somehow I knew that I was ready and would be strong enough to deal with whatever lay ahead. Afterwards as I discussed the experience with the rest of the group it felt like a clear premonition of great change on the way. As the weekend came to a close and I drove the long journey back to Galway, my thoughts drifted to a myriad of possibilities – a new job or relationship, maybe moving home. Nothing could have prepared me for what lay ahead.

A momentum had already taken hold of my life that I was totally unaware of. A few weeks later as I prepared to travel to the UK to attend a course for work, I had a strange experience. I was on my own in a meeting room trying to make contact with the organizers, but it was like I had entered a communications black hole. There were missed calls, wrong numbers, engaged tones and finally I just sat and waited. As I did, I scrolled through my mobile phone and came across an advertisement for a woman called Carmel Conway who was giving readings in Galway. Without giving it much thought I made an appointment for that coming weekend and went back to work. Although I didn't know it then, life was stepping in to help me. As I arrived for my appointment the following Saturday, I just knew that some greater force had brought me there. I was being prepared. Carmel talked of a very different life two or three years down the road and I felt a strong connection to her. Although I didn't realize it at the time, the session would end up sustaining me in what would be a few difficult years ahead. Just before I left, she pointed to my chest and said that she could see heaviness on the right-hand side. I don't remember any specific words of advice. I just felt hopeful for the first time in a long time. In February 2020, almost four years later to the day, Carmel reappeared in my life. Suffice to say, I now understand the connection between us and the future that she pointed to is starting to take shape.

At the time, I thought no more about her parting words. It was only a week later that they took on new meaning. I was reading in bed and I felt my arm brush against something hard. It was a lump in the exact position Carmel had pointed to and I felt a worrying sense of déjà vu. I pressed my fingers hesitantly against it, feeling its shape and size. The idea of cancer was far from my mind so I just pushed it to one side and went about my day. I wasn't ready to consider the possibility that something might be wrong. It hummed away in the back of my mind for a couple of weeks until I mentioned it to a colleague while travelling with work. She suggested that it might just be a cyst, but I wasn't experiencing any pain. A nagging voice stayed with me until I finally gave in and rang my GP. She gave me an appointment for the following day. I don't remember being very worried. Detached is the best way I can describe my state of mind as I drove there. Although it might sound strange, I felt like life had been slipping out of my grasp for quite some time and all I could do was just let go. After the examination, the doctor told me she was referring me to the local BreastCheck Clinic for a mammogram. Even then I didn't feel too worried as there was no history of cancer in my family. In my mind the word cancer and I just didn't go together in the same sentence. I didn't mention the appointment to anyone until I told my sister Orla the day before. I also told a friend, only because I had arranged to meet her for lunch on the same day as the mammogram. On some level I knew that once I said it out loud, it would become real and I wasn't yet ready for that.

In the meantime, I set off to the UK for my course. I got through the first day, but a rising sense of anxiety overwhelmed me and I had to leave early on the second day. I still don't know what happened except that I was almost paralyzed with fear. I felt like a fish out of water and deep down I knew the course was not for me. It was a world I no longer fit in or had any interest in. I had come to the end of that road, although I didn't know it at the time, and many miracles were conspiring to redirect the course of my life. As I left to fly home I felt a failure, yet the overwhelming feeling was one of relief. I didn't get long to dwell on it, as four days later I was sitting in a hospital gown in the BreastCheck Clinic back in Galway. I was shuttled quickly from mammogram to biopsy without time to digest what was happening. I had longed for change, but this wasn't what I had in mind. After the first biopsy had been taken of the breast tissue, the doctor inserted a second needle under my arm to biopsy the lymph nodes. The reality suddenly hit me that everything was definitely not okay. I felt the tension of the previous weeks bubble up and I started to cry. I will always remember the nurse who grabbed hold of my hand and smiled warmly at me. I wondered how many tears she must witness every day. You have gone well beyond the routine when you are having a biopsy and it takes its toll emotionally. I dried my eyes, got dressed and was called back to the consultation room. I hesitated as I didn't expect to get any official news. I didn't want any official news. I felt like I had been through enough for one day and I just wanted to run out the door before the bomb was dropped. As long as it wasn't verbalized, I could stay in my old world for a little while longer. That wasn't to be the case. After a few minutes the consultant appeared and quickly broke the news. The words were said in a matter-of-fact way but with great compassion. All I heard was chemotherapy, surgery, radiotherapy. The bomb was dropped. I had breast cancer. There was no going back.

I was left alone with a cancer support nurse who talked me through what lay ahead. Very little of what she said went in. All I could manage to ask was – *Am I going to lose my hair?* That to me was almost more devastating than the fact that I had cancer. It was a change that was going to drastically alter my physical appearance and would be impossible to hide. It would be the end of my old life as I knew it. The nurse hugged me as I left and told me to come back for the official biopsy results a week later. Although the consultant had enough experience with breast cancer and could recognize the signs, the biopsy would tell the type of breast cancer and the stage, thus determining the treatment plan. Still, there was no escaping the fact that it was cancer and chemotherapy, surgery and radiotherapy would be required. The message that stayed with me as I left the clinic was the importance of having a good support network. Cancer, (or more accurately, cancer treatment) as I later found out, strips you bare and leaves you feeling very vulnerable and raw. It is a very difficult journey to undertake on your own. I felt lucky that all of my family lived locally and I had good friends. I wondered what it must be like for someone to receive that news and not have any support around them. At the same time, I knew that I had lived a very independent life and there were only a small number of people that I felt comfortable confiding in. I had years of practice surviving on my own and I had always been reluctant to ask for help. As I stumbled out the side door of the clinic, blinded by tears, I was acutely aware of life going on as normal around me, yet I felt removed from it all. Traffic was backed up as it was lunchtime and people were rushing along to their next appointment of the day. As I made my way back to my car, I was glad that I had made plans to meet a good friend. I knew I could be myself with her and just let go. I was being looked after by a much greater power as I started to take in the news. It was going to take time to become accustomed to this new direction my life was taking.

Gift

I had longed for change and it was finally happening, although not as I had hoped or imagined. Looking back, I see that it couldn't have happened any other way. My experience with cancer was closing the door on a chapter of my life. It was also the beginning of a journey of great transformation that continues to this day.

Chapter 2

The Writing Was On The Wall

If you're not excited about it, it's not the right path.
Abraham Hicks

In saying *The writing was on the wall*, I mean there were many signs that my life was out of balance long before my diagnosis. I can honestly say that in the years leading up to it I was struggling. Although I had been passionate about my job for many years, I knew with every fiber of my being that it was time for change. Added to this, I had some questionable personal relationships in my life that were not serving me at all and only added to my distress. I continued to work very hard in an effort to shake off these feelings but to no avail. I found myself living with a constant low-level anxiety and sometimes all-out panic as I tried to maintain the façade of being okay. I was lost and I didn't know what to do. I felt like an actor in my own life. I was playing many roles but none of them were me.

In early November 2014 I had been involved in a car accident. Luckily, although no one was seriously injured, I was left feeling shattered. I was literally brought to a standstill and was on sick leave for a month. It felt like someone had tripped a switch in my brain. I realized that my body was telling me enough was enough. I was burnt out. I needed to change how I was living as it wasn't working for me anymore. I didn't listen, or in truth I didn't know what to do. On the day of the accident, I was feeling particularly stressed. I had always loved being out on the road meeting students and teachers. I felt like I was really making a difference, but something had changed. The financial crash of 2008 had put enormous pressure on everyone and in the public sector where I worked it was no different. Year on year it intensified and everyone was feeling stretched. Yet instinctively I also knew that it was time to broaden my horizons; to develop other skills and be of service in the world in a new way. I say this at the risk of sounding sorry for myself, but what I really want to illustrate is that the warning signs are always there. I had felt them creeping up on me for quite some time. Knowing what I now know, I won't do that again. Hindsight is a great teacher and I don't regret any of it. I had to recognize my limits in all aspects of my life and learn about boundaries. I needed to take my power back.

Returning to the car accident, it was a surreal experience. I was almost at the doorstep of the school that I was visiting when it happened. I drove straight into the back of a car at a pedestrian crossing. I can remember the seconds before it happened so well. I knew I was in the red zone in terms of stress. I was very agitated and couldn't concentrate. The last thing I remember was my attention straying to a woman pushing a buggy on the footpath nearby. I thought she looked so happy and relaxed and I envied her. In that moment I would have given anything to be in her shoes although I knew nothing of her life. I took my eyes and attention off the road. Then bang! Everything stopped. I don't remember the details except that it all seemed to be over within a matter of minutes. I gave my details to the Guards and then everyone dispersed. I was down in County Kerry, far from home, and my car was a write-off. As I started to panic I heard a knock on the window and I turned to see an elderly man with kind eyes looking in at me. He had witnessed the accident and invited me to his home to recover. I gladly accepted the offer. In their cozy kitchen that I still remember vividly, his wife made me a strong cup of sweet tea. As the sugar hit my system I managed to pull myself together. They helped me arrange the practical details of hiring a car and as it was going to take a few hours, they made plates of sandwiches and many pots of tea were consumed. As the afternoon passed, I found myself alone with the man's wife and we chatted easily. On entering the house I had noticed many photographs of a young boy who looked to be in his late teens. I asked her about him. With tears in her eyes, she proceeded to tell me that he was her son and he had been killed in a car accident a few years before. I could sense her grief was still very raw. She talked about him, his plans, his girlfriend and the life he had great hopes for. Then he was gone. Something happened during our conversation and it has stayed with me to this day. As we left for the car hire office we bumped into a neighbor. Hearing about the accident she quietly said to me that they were very special people. I couldn't have agreed with her more. I'm not sure what I would have done if they hadn't looked after me so well.

On the drive we talked more. She pointed to the graveyard where her son was buried. She told me that she hadn't been able to talk about him until today. We hugged as I left the car and I thanked her. I know that something very important happened between us in those few hours. She got the opportunity to open up to a stranger and hopefully got some relief. I felt huge gratitude that my accident hadn't been any worse and nobody had been seriously injured. You couldn't plan that situation. I have no doubt that the universe intervened. Here I was just after a car accident and the people who come to my rescue happened to have lost their own son in a car accident. I was acutely reminded of how precious life is and how it can all change in an instant. I left for home feeling privileged that she had been comfortable enough to share something so personal with me.

For the next few days I was wired and found it hard to sleep. Adrenaline was still coursing through my system. It was only when the effects wore off that I plummeted and found it hard to function. I didn't understand what was happening to me and broke down when I visited my GP. She told me it was shock and that the accident had shaken me up on many levels.

Looking back I can see that it was a breakdown of sorts. When I returned to work, I applied for different jobs in my desperation to make change. Deep down I knew it wasn't the solution. I just wasn't sure what else to do. I wasn't successful in my applications and I wasn't the least bit surprised. I was actually quite relieved. I ended up filling in a maternity leave cover, but this role didn't solve any of my problems. Things were rapidly going downhill. Although I had a good employer, I was finding it harder to reconcile my love of working with young people with my increasing desire to work more holistically and take on new challenges. I had embraced a holistic approach to my own life for many years before this. My efforts had only intensified after the breakup of my marriage as I tried to process all the pain. I explored different therapies, read self-help books and attended yoga and meditation retreats. I loved every minute of this aspect of my life. It felt very natural to me, yet I struggled to see where it would take me. I eventually trained as a sound healing therapist, undertook training in craniosacral therapy and completed a foundation course in counseling and psychotherapy. All the same, I always felt like I was dancing around making a life for myself using these skills. My life was split in two and the effort to keep both lives going was becoming more and more of a strain. I struggled to know what steps to take and fear was also holding me back. If I'm honest, I was afraid of what people might think; that they might judge or dismiss me for my interests. It is only in recent years that I have been able to own who I am and let go of the need for external validation. So as I left work for the Christmas holidays at the end of 2015, I vowed to myself that next year would be the year for change. I started the process by enquiring about training as a Bio-Energy therapist, but more training was not to be the answer. I had planned to start the course in April, but life had other plans for me.

Gift

The encounter after my car accident has stayed with me to this day. It was clearly a wake-up call, reminding me that life is precious. I should cherish it and trust my inner voice. The struggle I had been feeling for quite some time was a sign that something needed to change. I didn't know it at the time but I was going to get another even bigger wake-up call.

Chapter 3

Digesting The News

With everything that has happened to you, you can either feel sorry for yourself or treat what has happened as a gift. Everything is either an opportunity to grow or an obstacle to keep you from growing. You get to choose.
Wayne Dyer

Coming to terms with the fact that I had cancer didn't take much time. Aside from the initial shock, some part of me felt an overwhelming sense of relief that I could finally stop. Nothing was expected of me anymore. I could just give myself fully to whatever lay ahead, knowing that I was in good hands with the medical team. I was due back to the clinic a week later to get the official test results, so I had a bit of time to absorb the news and think of any questions about the proposed treatment plan. When I met with the consultant again, he confirmed that it was stage two breast cancer (estrogen receptor positive) and that it had spread to some of my lymph nodes. I was relieved to hear that it was the *common garden variety* as he put it and very treatable. He reassured me that I would be well looked after and had nothing to worry about. First up on the proposed treatment plan was eight weeks of chemotherapy with a month to recover. This would be followed by surgery and then about eight weeks later I would undergo twenty-five daily sessions of radiotherapy. He advised that I commence treatment within the next few weeks which gave me some time to prepare for what lay ahead.

I broke the news to family and a small number of friends. I felt a huge outpouring of support, but it still felt surreal. It was like talking about somebody else. Although I was relieved at the prospect of putting my life on pause for a while, I still experienced the full gamut of emotions that accompany a diagnosis like cancer. I seesawed between fear and acceptance on any given day. I could burst into tears one moment and a few minutes later be laughing out loud as I watched something funny on TV. There were times when I sank into the knowledge that I had cancer in my body and I was okay with it. There were other times when the reality became all too much. Then I would busy myself with anything that might distract from how I was feeling. I imagine this is quite a common reaction. Difficult life-changing news cannot be processed all at once. We digest it in bite-sized chunks and that is what I did. As I swung between denial and acceptance, the pockets of acceptance gradually filled up until eventually they became my predominant state. In saying that, there are still moments to this day when I have to remind myself that I had cancer. It is not because of denial anymore. Now almost five years on, it really feels like I have moved past my health challenge and all it had to teach me. My experience is that when we learn the lessons from anything that enters our life, it literally dissolves into thin air. So although I am passionate about sharing my story in the hope of helping others, cancer is not something which is now in my consciousness on a daily basis. Yet at the time I had to live through it and cope as best I could.

As I tried to prepare myself for whatever lay ahead, my interest in all things holistic led me to read many books on the topic. The first was *The Journey* by Brandon Bays. An American author and healer, she was diagnosed with a large tumor in her uterus in 1992. She decided to explore alternative means of healing before resorting to surgery and drugs. In her book she describes the extraordinary soul-searching, and ultimately freeing, journey of healing she went on. Just six and a half weeks after her diagnosis, she was pronounced perfectly healthy. Without the need for drugs or surgery, the tumor had disappeared. Her book and accompanying tapes take you on this journey, which as I understand it are intended to free you from the emotional and mental blocks that have led the body to become dis-eased. I also got to meet an amazing woman called Anita Moorjani. I was friends with the shaman who had run the retreat I attended at the beginning of the year and he introduced me to her. She had made a miraculous recovery from end-stage cancer and wrote a book about her experience called *Dying to Be Me*. As it happened she was hosting an event in Dublin in the coming days so I jumped at the opportunity to attend. It was a life-changing evening for me. I started listening to the audiobook in advance and I was so moved by it that I had finished it by the time I got to see her. I have no doubt that reading her book and meeting her in Dublin totally changed how I viewed my cancer diagnosis. She bravely shared her story, holding nothing back. In 2006, she had fallen into a coma as her four-year struggle with cancer was coming to an end. She had a near-death experience (NDE), and when she regained consciousness she was totally free of cancer within weeks. To give you a sense of how sick she was, she told us about tumors the size of lemons throughout her lymphatic system. Her organs had shut down and her brain was filled with fluid, as were her lungs. Her skin had developed lesions that were weeping toxins. The doctors told her husband that she would not make it through the night. When she did come out of the coma and made a complete recovery, her medical team was confounded by the fact that there was no trace of cancer or illness in her body. She showed us copies of the medical reports. She explained what she had experienced during the NDE and I have included a very short extract here in her own words (I would recommend reading this book, particularly if you are dealing with a cancer diagnosis):

I also understood that the cancer was not some punishment for anything I'd done wrong, nor was I experiencing negative karma as a result of any of my actions, as I'd previously believed. It was as though every moment held infinite possibilities, and where I was at that point in time was the culmination of every decision, every choice, and every thought of my entire life. Many fears and my great power had manifested this disease.

Both of these books communicate a really empowering message about the interconnectedness of our mind, body and spirit. Reading them left me in no doubt that our bodies are just a reflection of our inner state and are communicating with us all the time in an effort to bring us to a state of harmony and balance. We are all familiar with the knots in our stomach that accompany feeling anxious or the fatigue that comes from being burnt out by the demands of our daily lives. What if we live in this state for long periods of time? Surely it has to have some effect on our biology and health. Listening to Anita Moorjani, I had no doubt that my life choices and feelings about myself had brought me to this point. This was a profound realization which I found very liberating. If this was the case, I could make change and go on to live a very different type of life. There was a long road ahead and first I had to deal with the fact that I had cancer in my body. We left the hotel where the talk was on, and for the first time since my diagnosis I felt truly calm. I just knew that everything was going to be okay. Whatever lay ahead, I would get through it.

When I returned to Galway I was glad to have time on my own. I needed to absorb everything that had happened over the previous few weeks. I was living alone and looked forward to being able to close the front door behind me and have no interruptions. I hadn't always felt that way. I had moved into the house in 2006 and it had never felt like a home. It had only served as a reminder of how happy I had been when purchasing an apartment in Dublin after getting married. Anyone who has moved into a new home with a partner can identify with the excitement of making it your own and the fun of doing it together. You feel grown-up and full of hope for your life ahead, especially when you are in your twenties. I was feeling none of those things when I bought a three-bedroom house in Galway. That might sound ungrateful, but all the money in the world couldn't have compensated for how miserable I felt at the time. I had no enthusiasm for decorating it or creating a home. I was just going through the motions. Ten years later it took on a whole new meaning in my life that I could never have foreseen. The house that I had little interest in was soon to become my cherished sanctuary.

Time moved on and I started to feel pressure from the medical team to set a date for starting chemotherapy. This was with my best interests at heart, but I was conflicted on which route to go. Should I take some time and investigate alternative options? Could I take a holistic approach that was compatible with my attitude to life? Or should I just fire ahead and put my body through what was going to be a very rigorous course of treatment? Of course I would have jumped at any opportunity of avoiding it and I was feeling particularly worried about the side effects of chemotherapy. I knew they would be pretty harrowing. Everyone around me wanted the best for me, yet I felt very torn. I knew that whatever decision I made, it had to be mine. It was my life and I needed to be sure and fully commit to it.

Gift

Meeting Anita Moorjani and hearing her story was life-changing. I knew that my illness was not some random happening but a culmination of many things in my life. It was empowering to know this and know that I could change. I felt a germ of hope take root inside.

Chapter 4

Taking Ownership

It's only as you take ownership for your life that you discover how powerful you truly are.
Allanah Hunt

The next few weeks were agonizing and the date that I was due to start chemotherapy was fast approaching. My head was bursting with information and the more I talked about it the more confused I got. I felt like I was rapidly running out of time and I didn't want to make the wrong decision. It might sound like there was no decision to be made, but that is not how it felt to me. Whatever treatment I underwent, I had to do it wholeheartedly. Life experience had taught me that acting like a victim would not serve me at all. I knew I had the capacity for great inner strength having come through other challenging times. I had to take ownership. It was my life and my responsibility. During this time a few things happened that turned out to be a godsend. They helped me get clarity and fully commit to whatever lay ahead. I know that when I resist and do things reluctantly, it is an uphill battle, and when it feels right and I am at ease, life flows. I believe, particularly when it comes to cancer treatment, if we can let go of fear and embrace it as much as possible, we feel empowered and as a result we contribute to the healing process.

I had made initial enquiries about Bio-Energy training before my diagnosis, so I decided to contact the organizers to explain that I wouldn't be going ahead. I ended up having a conversation with a very understanding woman who worked there. I told her about my diagnosis, the treatment I would undergo and also about my fear of losing my hair. I know many women have had to deal with this reality and all cope with it differently. It may seem like a small problem in the overall scheme of what was happening, but it was the only thing I could relate to at the time. In the course of our conversation she told me about her experience with alopecia and how devastating it had been. She too had long curly hair like me. She explained that losing it was not just about losing her hair. It was like losing part of her identity. I could totally relate to that. However, the most important thing I remember her saying, was how liberating and ultimately life-changing it ended up being. Although that might sound over the top, it ended up being true for me too. I was also fortunate because my hair did start to grow back a few months after chemotherapy finished. With alopecia there is no certainty that it will ever grow back. As we ended our conversation, she shared a prayer with me.

Help direct and guide me on the right path. Present me with the right people, places and opportunities so that I may fulfill my soul's purpose. And I give thanks for everything I have and for everything you are about to send me.

She said it had helped her surrender to what was happening in her own life. I felt buoyed up after our conversation. I started to say it every day and gradually I could feel things starting to shift. There is a time for research, conversations and gathering information to help you make a decision in life, but there is also a time to trust your inner wisdom – the unseen intelligent force that animates all life. Whatever name you want to give it – intuition, higher power, universal mind, God, source, the infinite – it doesn't really matter. It is beyond definition. I experience it as a powerful, loving energy that is available to me in every moment, especially when I am still. It is a supportive guiding force in my life. It takes care of life. Consciously connecting with this energy is the reason why I meditate. It knows the big picture, which I don't. It has changed everything for me. It is an anchor in my life. It is the source of inspiration and creativity in my life. It is the source of my peace and contentment. Have you ever gone against your instincts although every fiber of your being told you not to? Have you dismissed a powerful feeling about something and regretted it? When we put too much emphasis on the external world and the constant stream of information and opinion, we give away our power. I knew it was time to go within.

Around this time I received a letter from the hospital with my date for starting chemotherapy. It was now only a week away. A friend called me to see how I was doing and I told her that I felt torn. I was struggling to commit to the treatment, but at the same time my gut was telling me it was the right thing to do. She referred me to chiropractor and healer, Dr. Yvonne Murphy, and said that she was very gentle in her work. Although she wouldn't tell me what to do it might bring me some clarity. I contacted Yvonne and as she was in India we arranged an initial session by Skype. Yvonne has over thirty years of experience working as a chiropractor and helping people heal from illness on all levels. I find it hard to put into words what happened during the treatment, but at the end of the session I felt much lighter and clearer. I had connected with a higher intelligence that was supporting me every step of the way. I just knew the right thing to do. I had no more doubt or fear.

In Yvonne's own words:

I have been using my sixth sense all my life. I was healed from a life-threatening condition 30 years ago by asking the Great Mystery for help. This developed into Medical Intuition during my 20 years of busy chiropractic work, where I specialized in pediatrics, cranial, birth trauma release and animal adjusting. My work has evolved over the past 25 years into a unique way of healing called Divine Clearing, because I found other approaches too narrow.

I knew there and then that I was making the right decision. Yvonne gently pointed out that going through cancer treatment may be necessary for me, not just in terms of physically healing, but also in terms of my personal growth and who I would be in the future. I can say for sure that is the case. I wouldn't be the person I am today if it wasn't for everything I went through. I speak now from personal experience and it is this experience which helps me connect with others and be of service in whatever way I can. I continue to see Yvonne regularly to this day.

Gift

Both of those encounters reminded me that if I trust myself and listen to my intuition, I will be okay. There is a time for research and information, but there is also a time to go quiet and listen. The answer is always inside.

Chapter 5

Welcoming Healing

Your living is determined not so much by what life brings to you as by the attitude you bring to life; not so much what happens to you as by the way your mind looks at what happens.
Kahlil Gibran

I'll always remember the morning of my first chemotherapy session. As I waited at home for my sister Orla to pick me up and drive me to the hospital, I sat in my kitchen and gazed out the window. The spring sunshine lit up the back garden and for a split second it could have been any other morning of my life as I prepared for work. At that moment, the life I had been longing to escape was now looking quite attractive. I shed a few tears as the tension of the previous weeks overwhelmed me. Whatever illusion of control I had felt over any aspect of my life was now well and truly gone. I was due at the hospital at 8:00am and when we arrived, my sister-in-law Sheila joined me and stayed for the day. I was looked after all the way. I had no idea what to expect and it was no accident that the very first person I set eyes on was a neighbor. He too was dealing with cancer and he waved to me as I approached. It was good to see a familiar face although it took me a few minutes to recognize him without his thick head of dark wavy hair. He smiled warmly at me, totally unconscious of his now shiny bald head. I would find out for myself a few weeks later that losing all your hair can be a truly liberating experience. Once registered at the main office I was directed to the waiting room. I had been warned that chemotherapy was a full-day affair even though the drugs are usually administered over a couple of hours. Blood tests are taken and there are a lot of checkups to make sure that your body is strong enough to withstand the side effects of treatment. It takes its toll as time goes on. The sound of laughter spilled out on to the corridor as I approached and it was easy to identify the chemotherapy veterans when I entered the room. The cannulas were a giveaway. People chatted easily as breakfast was served from a trolley, exchanging supportive smiles with anyone new like me. Once the blood tests were approved a few hours later, I was set up in a room with three other women. As I watched the toxic infusion enter my system to do its work, I was so grateful for the distraction of their company. It was a surreal experience. We might as well have been at the hairdressers as we chatted easily and shared our worries about hair loss and other things. I had been told that my hair would start to fall out somewhere between the second and third treatment and I was dreading it. I still couldn't imagine functioning without it. What struck me that day, and every other day I went for treatment, was the honest and open way that people interacted with each other. There was no drama or hysterics, just an acceptance of what was happening and an attitude of dealing with it as normally as possible. It was in sharp contrast to other aspects of my life, where there was plenty of drama. The irony wasn't lost on me. I knew people who had all the external trappings of a good life but didn't seem very contented. On some level I looked forward to being part of this new club each time I went for treatment. I experienced a wonderful feeling of belonging that I hadn't felt in a very long time. It really brought home to me the power of community to prop us up during hard times.

I could recount many stories of little kindnesses and support that I received during the three months of chemotherapy. Instead I'll just mention a few that stood out. One day a friend offered to take the day off work and spend it with me in the hospital. I had to be there for 8:00am and it could be 3:00pm or later before I was ready to go home, so it was a generous offer. Although I often felt groggy when the drugs were administered, we still chatted and laughed. She told me it was one of the most enjoyable days she had spent in a long while and a nice break from work. It struck me how crazy life was, if a day on the oncology ward was a nice escape. I'm not denying the incredibly difficult treatments people were undergoing. It just reminded me that life is not really about what happens to us but more about the attitude we choose to bring to it. The attitude of everyone I met was optimistic, accepting and full of gratitude for being alive. One particular day I was in a smaller two-bed room for treatment. The lady sharing the room with me was very chatty and as we talked she proceeded to tell me about her own situation. She had breast cancer initially, but the latest scan showed that it had spread and was now in her brain. She had been told that it was inoperable. She would soon start a new experimental treatment although she had been given a poor prognosis. Despite her circumstances, she was a gregarious woman. Throughout the morning she took a number of phone calls. She later told me they were work-related as she was chairperson of a local organization. I was struck by all the plans she was making in the midst of what she was going through. It was obvious she was passionate about making a difference in her community. Doing what she loved kept her going, she explained to me. Later that day I developed an allergic reaction to a drug called Taxol. It was a new drug that I was starting for the second stage of treatment. I started hyperventilating and was moved to a room on my own to recover. When I came round, the same lady called in. She was on her way home and just wanted to check that I was doing okay before she left. I was struck by our encounter and her concern for my welfare.

As the months passed, I was lucky enough to meet many great people I would never have encountered in my former life. One particular woman, who was always accompanied by her daughter, was on maintenance chemotherapy. She explained that she had a port inserted in her chest so that treatment could continue at home as well as in the hospital. Dealing with cancer in her lungs and bowel had been her life for the past three years. It was now just part of her daily routine. Again, I was amazed by her attitude. She smiled and explained that she felt lucky. It allowed her to go away for a night or visit friends. On my last day of treatment she gave me a candle and told me that she had included my name in a novena she was attending near her home. I have never seen her since that day, but I will always remember her. Not once in hospital did I hear anyone complain about their situation, even though it would be totally understandable if they did. It felt like cancer had washed away all the pointless worries and complaints we get knotted up in every day. The focus had shifted to embracing life, being present and connecting with other human beings. I hope that I never forget the valuable life lessons I was being taught. I realized that the most important thing that we can give another human being is our time and attention. It is extremely healing to be listened to and truly seen by another person. I really believe that many of life's problems would disappear if we remembered this. When your life is threatened and everything falls apart, nothing else matters.

Gift

I have no control over what happens to me, but I do have control over my attitude and how I respond. Every patient I met in hospital inspired me with their attitude. I have no doubt that healing was taking place on many levels. It was not just down to the physical treatments being administered. It was because of the genuine, loving, human connections taking place.

Chapter 6

Feminine Wisdom

The repression of the feminine has led to a planet on the edge of collapse. The re-emergence is going to be a dance to behold.
Clare Dakin

The words of Clare Dakin were written long before we knew anything about the pandemic that would sweep across the world in a matter of weeks in early 2020. We might consider her wisdom as we unite to recalibrate, rebuild and figure out how to live in a more balanced and healthy way. I had been given this message loud and clear when I navigated my encounter with breast cancer only a few years before. From the day I was diagnosed, right through to the present day, many incredibly strong women entered my life. It is no accident that my experience with breast cancer coincided with meeting them. It started with my introduction to chiropractor, Dr. Yvonne Murphy, just before I started chemotherapy, and continues to this very day where I am surrounded by many like-minded women. I would not be where I am without their support, encouragement and inspiration. I found my tribe. They have reminded me of the powerful feminine qualities of creativity, love, intuition, empathy and sensitivity, qualities that I had lost touch with. I believe we have reached that time on the planet too. A patriarchal social system that glorifies only the qualities of logic, intellect, action and judgment is no longer sustainable. Without the balance of both male and female energies we suffer and we have seen how our world does too.

Masculine energy is outward, action-oriented and mind-driven. Female energy is more inward, reflective and heart-oriented. We all possess both whether we are male or female. However, the heart-mind connection has become disconnected for many of us, and as a result we often view the world through a mind of separation and judgment. It has been one of my greatest personal challenges to abstain from judgment. I know that when I judge others it is stemming from insecurity on my part. I am feeling hurt or frustrated about something and my ego lashes out from a place of fear. I don't criticize myself anymore when I do it. I know it is part and parcel of being a human being. It just means that I am out of balance and need to re-center and connect with my heart. We balance our masculine and feminine aspects when we connect our minds with our hearts. Although we still hear stories of prejudice and oppression from around the world, I believe we are entering a healing time on the planet, a time when the feminine will no longer be suppressed and undermined. The challenge is that we have to see and acknowledge the darkness before we can heal and move on from it. It is painful but we will get through it. This applies to mother nature too as we start to show a newfound respect for our environment and the beautiful planet that is our home. As I was surrounded by women and their nurturing qualities, I started to embrace that side of myself, an aspect which I had neglected for far too long. Although I wasn't conscious of it at the time, I had been living exclusively from my masculine energy. Through the circumstances of my life, I was a survivor and very independent. I pushed myself hard and gave the impression that nothing really bothered me. I acted like I didn't need support and was quite self-sufficient. Nothing could have been further from the truth. This was just my survival instinct kicking in during difficult times. I didn't know how to embrace my softer side and indeed was afraid to. My illness was showing me how out of balance my life had become. I needed to address it. According to yoga philosophy, the male energy channel is on the right side of the body and the feminine is on the left. It is no accident that breast cancer manifested on the right side of my body.

It was also very important to me that I deal with cancer in a very holistic way, nursing my body, mind and spirit. I looked to herbalism, nutrition, natural therapies, exercise, counseling and spiritual healing for support. Again, it was women who just naturally showed up to help me because that is what I needed. I know that if I had just undergone conventional medical treatments, I wouldn't be where I am today, doing what I am doing. I took an active role in my own healing. My experience was one of collaboration where I sought out interventions that addressed all aspects of my illness. The medical treatments are designed to cure the physical symptoms of cancer, but it is an illness that goes far beyond its physical manifestation. We have to go on that journey deep inside ourselves if we are to truly heal and live a healthy life. The body is the last place that symptoms of imbalance show up. Physical symptoms are the language of the body. My sense is that physical illness starts a lot earlier and may be experienced as feeling stuck, depressed, anxious or unhappy. It will ultimately manifest in the body at some point unless we take action. The word disease comes from dis-ease. So I would encourage you to pay attention to those aspects of your life that feel out of balance. You don't have to get cancer or any other illness to wake up, heal and thrive.

While I was in hospital for surgery, I shared a ward with about eight women. It was a blessing that I wasn't in a room on my own as I would have missed the company, support and humor of the women that I met and still remember to this day. A few days before I was due to go home, a lady in her eighties called Maura was moved to the bed next to me. She had just undergone a very grueling operation on her bowel and as the nurses moved her during the night I could hear her cries of pain. I really felt for her. The next morning after breakfast, the curtain that separated us was pulled back to reveal a tiny, fragile lady tucked up in bed. Despite her great discomfort Maura smiled at me and warmly engaged in conversation. She turned out to be one of the funniest, wisest women I had ever met. Even in her poor physical condition, her life force was strong and I sensed a bright light shining from her. We laughed, shared stories and I connected easily with her. I admire the fact that she chose to undergo a very difficult operation with such courage and optimism and without a trace of self-pity. I left hospital with the conviction that this was the type of woman I wanted to emulate in the future, and I felt very grateful that I had the opportunity to spend time with her. On the day I was leaving I gave her a copy of Anita Moorjani's book – *Dying to Be Me*. It had shifted my perspective on cancer and life completely. I wanted to pass it on to someone who was ready to hear that message too.

Every woman I met reminded me that it is possible to live powerfully while also being gentle and warm. It is through our vulnerability that we display our strength. I had seen many women operating predominantly from their masculine energy, particularly in my working life. This isn't a criticism. They were doing their best to function in a male-dominated system. I tried to fit in too, but it wasn't me. There was no room in the system for the power of the feminine. Now that we are living in a totally altered world, I hope we see more women find their voice. I hope we see more women step into their personal power in a way that honors who they truly are. I hope we see more women collaborate rather than compete. I hope we embrace a new way of being in the world that honors the harmony of masculine and feminine qualities. For far too long we have lived in a world that is out of balance. True feminine strength is about getting in touch with our inner wisdom and insight. It is a strength that is about openness, vulnerability, compassion, flexibility, non-judgment and intuitive wisdom. They are qualities that our world is crying out for right now. I now look to people who embody these qualities. I endeavor to learn from them. The planet urgently needs us to come back into balance and cherish the feminine.

Gift

Through all the amazing women I meet every day, I am shown the true power of the feminine. It is a power that we all benefit from embracing whether we are male or female. Now is the time for more compassion, love, healing, understanding and harmony in the world as we navigate this next stage of our evolution.

Chapter 7

Longed-For Silence

The inspiration you seek is already within you. Be silent and listen.
Rumi

As time passed, and particularly during chemotherapy, an overwhelming sense of stillness entered my life. This sense of peace has mostly continued to this day and I'm very grateful for it. In fact I need a lot of quiet. Like most people, I lived a life full of noise and activity. Whether it was TV, radio, social media, noisy environments or my job, which involved a lot of talking, I had found it exhausting. I also had a mind that was constantly chattering and worrying needlessly. I longed for silence and had often dreamt of just packing up and going far away.

Going through chemotherapy changed all that. It is like entering a bubble. Everything stops as you move from one appointment to the next. I had nothing to plan or organize other than to turn up on time. It took a bit of adjustment and I often tried to do more than I was able for afterwards. However, as the cumulative effects of each chemotherapy session took their toll, I had no choice but to give in. My body needed time to heal and recover as did my mind. I developed a new appreciation for my body and thought of the many times I had abused it and pushed it very hard. I was happy to rest. My mind took longer to calm down as I had spent much of my life consumed with past experiences or projecting into the future. I found it almost impossible to stay in the present as I was afraid of what I might meet. Distraction was my best friend.

Throughout treatment I lived alone in my house and I was grateful for that. Family and friends were wonderful, visiting and dropping in food, but I found it very hard to be in company for long. The effort it took to make conversation was exhausting. I loved the quiet in the house and I followed meditation tapes, read and watched a lot of inspiring videos on personal growth and transformation. I found that as well as living in a quiet environment, I was becoming quieter inside. My mind started to slow down and I felt its grasp on me loosen. I learnt that I am not my thoughts and I stopped paying as much attention to them. In the words of spiritual teacher, Mooji – *Thought by itself has no power. It is only your belief in a thought that gives it life.* I was learning that the chatter of my mind only held the power that I chose to give it. I was starting to wake up and see that there was another way of being in the world. Although there are still plenty of times when I worry and overthink, I have new awareness and I don't tend to get consumed by negative thoughts in the way that I used to. I'm learning to observe and redirect to more supportive thoughts. As we know, where attention goes, energy flows. Whatever we put our energy on gains momentum and grows. We really do have the power to believe things into existence and I for one would prefer that they are things that I want.

Living with more silence may sound like a luxury, or in fact impossible, particularly when you are working and may have a family and children to look after. I had struggled with this dilemma although I didn't have children. However, I did have a full-on job, travelling, giving presentations, and being in a noisy work environment. I was very good at keeping busy and found it very hard to switch off. In truth, I was afraid to switch off. I associated being quiet with meeting pain and I didn't want to relive that feeling under any circumstance. As a result, I often felt overwhelmed and the only solution I could imagine was to drop out of life altogether; I know, not very practical for most people. Over the years I had attended many yoga and meditation retreats and although it was a struggle at the beginning, my mind would gradually start to slow down. However, I had not yet managed to bring this practice into my daily life. I always returned to my old ways.

A few years earlier I had attended a day-long, silent retreat in a Buddhist meditation center near home. I remember the feelings of anxiety as I drove there. I couldn't imagine spending a full day in total silence. I worried about old emotions coming to the surface and not being able to escape. Instead, I found the atmosphere open and welcoming and the day was broken into short sessions with breaks and walking meditations. Although the whole day was conducted in silence, it wasn't overwhelming. I never imagined that eating lunch with a group of people in silence could be such a pleasant experience, but it was. There were no expectations, just a feeling of community and peace. As I left the center that evening, I felt relaxed and glad that I had gone. However, even more revealing was how I felt in the following days. My life ran more smoothly and I didn't get as worried about things that would normally knock me off-center. I realized that the effects of meditation are not always felt in the moment. Instead, they have a ripple effect in our lives. With regular practice, we start to feel the benefit, and as a result the world feels the benefit. There is a reason it is called a meditation practice. It is only by meditating consistently that I noticed my life take on a whole new meaning and rhythm.

I started to understand that it doesn't really matter how active and busy my life is, it is more about what is happening inside. When I feel calm and peaceful, I bring that to what I do and who I meet. It changes the encounter. We have all met people whose company we have found very calming, and the opposite, where we felt agitated or drained after the encounter. The point is, we can only bring to the world what we have inside, and yet our inner life is the one that we are most inclined to ignore. In our modern, busy world it definitely isn't easy to stay grounded in a place of calm. Constant activity is admired, while little emphasis is placed on the impact of living from a place of stillness and peace. I always believed my value was determined by how much I was *doing*. I'm glad to have had that view challenged, for I had reached my limits. I had to find another way. I believe that the state of the world is just a reflection of the state of our minds and the benefits would be far-reaching if we all embraced more stillness in our lives.

Through my illness, I came to know and value silence. There is a time for action, but when I come from a place of internal quiet rather than agitation, I feel better overall. I make better decisions, I speak less, I take time to listen and I am less judgmental. I connect with my inner guidance and trust it. I discovered a spacious, creative place within and decisions now come more easily. I feel guided without the need to overthink and overplan. I am learning to trust my inner compass. I no longer feel the need to endlessly discuss and weigh up options and worry. In fact, I avoid it. I have a better feeling of being in flow or more in tune with the rhythm of life. It's hard to describe. I just know when something feels right and I know when it doesn't. I had spent a lot of time running around in mindless activity, with much of it contributing little to my life. Now, more often than not, my activity is coming from a place of calm and purpose. I hope that as a result, I make a more positive contribution to the world. In saying this, I don't want to sound like my life runs smoothly all the time. It definitely does not. I panic, get anxious and revert to my old habits of trying to control life. However, now I know there is another way and when I stop and get silent I can usually find it. As an example, after I wrote the first draft of this book, I put it to one side. I wanted to give it time to settle. Life then took a totally unexpected turn and I went on to publish my first novel, *The Tapestry of Life*. That definitely wasn't planned. I stopped for a while after that. I had no idea what to do next. I didn't have a project lined up, which is very unusual for me. I was often asked if I was writing again. People encouraged me to start a new book, yet deep down I knew it was not the right time. I wanted to get back to finishing this book. I sat tight for a few weeks and wondered how I might get a publisher who would be a good fit for my story. Not long after, I noticed the *Writers' & Artists' Yearbook and Diary* in a bookshop and it also popped up on my social media feed. I knew instinctively this was where I needed to start. I spent the next couple of months writing submissions to publishers and agents and I felt confident that it would all work out. There were a few months of no responses and I wondered if it had been a waste of time. Yet I stuck with it and made more submissions. I just knew I wasn't done and that the right publisher would show up and they did. An offer came in from one of the later submissions which I was delighted to accept. Even if I had not received an offer of a contract, I know that I would have been okay. I would eventually understand why things had worked out the way they did. Now I try to live my life like this every day, taking my cues from what shows up. I know that everything, whether I like it or not, is happening to help me. I may wake up with an idea of what I plan to do that day, but if I feel an intuitive nudge to do something else, then I will go in a different direction. Obviously, if I have a meeting or have made arrangements, I follow through with them. I have worked hard to create a simpler life. It is a life of ups and downs, like everyone's, but it is the life I have chosen to live. I have found a way of working that is more fluid and creative and it is just right for me. I feel more on track than I ever have.

Gift

I am very grateful for the gift of silence in my life. It is a work in progress as am I. Now I feel a sense of flow, whereas in the past I often felt stuck and frustrated. Through the many days of fatigue and exhaustion, the quiet place inside revealed itself and it has completely changed me.

Chapter 8

Being Connected

In the tapestry of life, we are all connected. Each one of us is a gift to those around us, helping each other be who we are, weaving a perfect picture together.
Anita Moorjani

I had been told that my hair would start falling out sometime after the second chemotherapy treatment, and I was feeling more uneasy with the passing of each day as I waited for the inevitable to happen. Although a gradual process, once it starts it is very stressful. My scalp became extremely sensitive and I watched as a few stray loose hairs quickly turned into large clumps being flushed down the toilet on a daily basis. Eventually, feeling like I was trying to hold back the tide, I resigned myself to the inevitable. I made an appointment with The Wig Clinic in Galway to get advice. Miriam, who runs the clinic, was a hairdresser for many years before she chose to help those suffering from hair loss. She was so sensitive and I felt completely understood from the moment I met her. She knows how distressing it is to not only cope with hair loss but also with the trauma that has caused it. I assumed that she would recommend chopping it off straight away. Instead, she advised waiting until I didn't look like me anymore. *It will be quite traumatic if you do it too soon,* she counseled wisely. When the day finally came, she was so right. At that stage I was well and truly ready. My hair no longer looked or felt like my own. I had already picked a wig that I could wear home, a welcome security blanket until I was ready to share my news with the world. As I left her clinic I took one last look at the remnants of my old life scattered on the floor. It was a poignant moment as I knew I was saying goodbye to an aspect of myself forever. Still, overall the experience was strangely cathartic, which I hadn't expected. I felt naked and vulnerable, and at the same time liberated. It was like shedding layers of clothes that had been weighing me down. Suddenly, I could see myself properly. This person was someone I was going to have to get to know and it would take some time.

My hair loss really felt like an outward reflection of change that was starting to happen internally. I was at the beginning of a journey to a new relationship with myself although I didn't understand it at the time. I used to hide behind my hair. It was my protection against the world. I preferred to blend in and was afraid to be seen. As it happened I hardly wore my wig. It was like trying to turn back the clock. I was warming to the new person being revealed and I didn't want to hide anymore. I was enjoying getting to know and really see myself properly for the first time. As I started developing a stronger sense of self, I felt more rooted and contented. I had a very tangible sense of being connected to a powerful energy, something that was outside of me but also inside. As much as possible, I put some structure on my day and created new habits and routines. I had time to really focus on me. I continued to develop my meditation practice in an effort to quiet my mind. I was voraciously reading books and following teachers on the subject of personal development and spiritual growth. I still do. My favorite while going through treatment was Wayne Dyer, and his teachings deeply affected me. I started writing. I began by documenting the progress of my treatment. It evolved into journaling, and then on the promptings of my friend Margie, it culminated in this book. I had no idea where it would all lead at the time. The catalyst for writing was the need to express myself and process what was happening. Soon I realized it could be more than that. Ultimately, I hoped that by sharing my experience, others might benefit from what I was starting to learn and continue to learn every day.

A few months after treatment I developed early-stage lymphedema in my right arm. My lymphatic system had been compromised and I was told that it could be triggered at any stage in life or maybe not at all. Forgetting that I needed to keep my right arm free of constriction, I wore a ring on Christmas day. It was late in the afternoon when I noticed the slightly bloated appearance of my arm. I was due back to the physiotherapist straight after Christmas, so thankfully it was caught early. She gave me exercises to do and I started seeing a specialist in lymphatic drainage. I also wore a compression sleeve when I was using my arm for anything strenuous. I really disliked wearing it. I found it uncomfortable and very unattractive-looking. I was angry with the world. I had just come through cancer treatment and then to be landed with this. It may seem a small price to pay, but when you have been through the ringer the slightest thing can bring you down. Interestingly, I noticed that flare-ups always happened when I had put additional stress on my system. The stress could be either physical, like overdoing it in the garden, or emotional, when I was feeling overwhelmed or anxious about something. It turned out to be a good barometer of my overall well-being and still is. It is my alarm system signaling when I need to slow down. I was encouraged to go to aqua-fit classes, so I joined The Ardilaun Leisure Club which was right on my doorstep. Going there soon became a valuable part of my rehabilitation routine. I looked forward to the classes as they gave a focus to my day. I met new people, some of them cancer survivors who were also finding their way like me. I got swimming lessons and surprised myself by becoming quite a competent swimmer. It felt like a moving meditation as my body and mind synchronized. As a result of regular swimming I stopped wearing the compression sleeve. When I got stronger I progressed to using the gym. After a couple of years of fatigue and very little activity, I could feel my body coming alive again and I started to appreciate it in a way that I never had. My focus now is on nourishing it and becoming strong, not pushing it just to look good. I took an interest in nutrition and I started listening to what my body wanted for fuel. I became sensitive to certain foods and made an appointment with a kinesiologist. He tested me for food intolerances to identify what was aggravating my body and causing inflammation. I adjusted my diet and now try to eat food in as natural a form as possible. He also tested my adrenal glands and told me that I was suffering from adrenal fatigue. Many years of stress and burnout had depleted them. I was actually relieved to hear that, as to this day I can still be hit with bouts of fatigue that floor me and frustrate me. I had never experienced this before cancer. I always had the resources to dig deep and keep going. It has been a good lesson in knowing my limits. On good advice, I got selective about listening to the news which is often full of doom and gloom. I kept myself informed, but I decided to focus on listening to positive messages that lifted my spirits. I was nurturing myself like I never had and it is a habit that has served me so well since.

As I was growing and changing I noticed that my relationships were changing. My connection with others was shifting like the connection with myself. This was not down to any conscious decision on my part. It just happened. New people appeared and others left. Illness is an eye-opener and sometimes those you thought you could rely on aren't able to show up for you, while others you least expect end up being the rock you can lean on. I was showing up in a different way and my relationships were too. I no longer had the energy to sustain those that drained me. It was only when I started to have a good relationship with myself that I started to see the unhealthy ones in my life and how I had contributed to them. Unhealthy relationships don't happen without our permission. Whatever pain or discomfort I had felt was there for a reason. I was rejecting myself by allowing them. Once I realized this, those relationships disappeared. It really was that simple. I truly believe that healthy relationships can only blossom in our lives when we have a healthy one with ourselves. Watch the movie that is playing out on the screen of your life and you get a good indication of the tape that you are playing inside. *As within, so without,* I kept reminding myself. I no longer wanted to be a victim and I became very attracted to people who were grounded and really taking ownership of their lives.

One day in the supermarket I felt my energy dipping and knew I needed to get home. As I approached the cashier to pay for my groceries, I dropped a six pack of water and I struggled to pick it up. A woman in the queue behind me noticed what had happened and offered to carry my bags. As we walked to the car I told her why I was so weak. As it turned out she lived quite close to me and she offered to go shopping for me whenever I needed. I left with her phone number, but as it turned out we didn't meet again. However, in that moment we connected and I was very grateful. It is said that people come into our lives for a reason, a season or a lifetime and I believe that. We never know it at the time. Some people we meet briefly and they teach us something or help us in some way; others may be with us for a while, maybe a work colleague or romantic relationship, and then there are people who are with us forever. It is our relationships that make up the tapestry that is our lives. I only had a brief encounter with the woman in the supermarket, yet she turned up just when I needed her help. I can see that every person I have met has contributed to who I am now, and the painful experiences probably more so. Now I really value my relationship with myself and I have a new appreciation for all relationships in my life. Before cancer I was so busy being busy that I found it hard to be present for others. From my experience, showing up from a place of connection to the stillness inside brings a deeper and richer quality to my relationships.

Gift

When illness forced me to spend time alone, I discovered a whole new relationship with myself. I connected with the quiet place inside. As a result, I have authentic, healthier relationships in my life. Above all, I feel a great sense of peace in my own company that I never enjoyed before.

Chapter 9

Surrounded By The Right People

Surround yourself only with people who are going to take you higher.
Oprah Winfrey

I was very conscious early on that I would need a good support system in place. This included family and friends, but I also knew that I would need to call on professionals to help me cope on what can be a very lonely journey. From past experience I knew there was always the possibility that I could sink to a place of despair and feel a victim of life. This was not the person I wanted to be. Don't get me wrong, there were many times I felt lost, yet deep down I knew that cancer had the potential to transform my life in really positive ways. Some part of me had already made that choice. I was starting to shed old Celine, and although I didn't know it at the time, cancer was to be the birthing ground of my new life.

One of the first things I did was make contact with Cancer Care West, the cancer support center in Galway city. I made an appointment to see their counselor very shortly after I was diagnosed. I felt uplifted straight away when I walked in the door. The premises were bright and airy and the staff welcomed me like an old friend. Oncology nurses were available to discuss any aspect of treatment and I was offered a range of holistic therapies to support me. I became a regular visitor there and I really looked forward to meeting others who were in the same boat as me. It was wonderful to be in an environment where I could just be myself and no explanation was needed. Being around people who are going through the same experience is very therapeutic. I attended a fantastic nutrition course and I always left on a high. There was lots of laughter and banter as we enjoyed a brief interlude from the world of cancer treatment. At the same time, I didn't want to surround myself only with people working in the field of cancer or dealing with a cancer diagnosis. I didn't want it to define me. It can be difficult being surrounded by illness when you are sick yourself. I had regular appointments with chiropractor and healer, Dr. Yvonne Murphy, so that I could support my healing and integrate all that I was experiencing. I returned to my psychotherapist, Sheila Glynn, who I had been seeing on and off since my car accident. She knew me before my cancer diagnosis so it was easier to pick up on this latest installment in my story. I sought advice from GP and medical herbalist, Dr. Dilis Clare, who is a leading authority on herbal medicine in Europe. She designed a treatment of herbs that would support my organs and body during chemotherapy, but most importantly she listened to me as a human being and not a collection of symptoms. I felt truly seen. I went for relaxing reflexology treatments and massages, particularly when my body was very low. I availed of a lovely pampering makeup session, organized by the Daffodil Centre in the hospital. This was shortly after surgery and when I really needed a lift concerning my appearance. I attended seminars and talks about dealing with cancer holistically. I was hungry to learn more about empowering approaches to life and it continues to this day. I wanted to be alert to all the guidance I was receiving. I just knew that cancer wasn't a random happening. It was a clear sign that I needed to change my life. I had been feeling that way for a long time before my diagnosis. Now was the time.

I started to learn that I'm always creating through my thoughts and feelings (my energetic signature). I attract based on who I am being, not what I want. That was a big shift in my understanding of life. I am not powerless. I was seeing this with my own eyes. I was feeling and thinking differently for lots of reasons, and my world was starting to look very different. I knew that I needed to be around kindred spirits who I connected with and they turned up. I could write a list of new people who just appeared in my life at the right time, with the right words or actions. I had wonderful conversations and spent time with old friends and new. I would have been lost without all of them. I was going through a difficult period in my life, but I didn't want sympathy. I felt supported and understood, and because of that I could be myself. I had so little energy that I developed a keen radar for unhealthy situations that would drain me and I avoided them. It has been a great life lesson. It is a lesson that was hammered home during my training to be a life coach. I learnt that I am creating my life by the choices I make in every moment. Every choice moves me towards or away from balance. When I choose to say *No* to certain things, it makes space for me to say *Yes* to others. Otherwise life can feel overwhelming. The idea that *No* is a complete sentence was very foreign to me. I had found it extremely difficult to say *No* all my life. I had never understood the importance of balance as I was an all or nothing person. It was something I was going to have to learn. So when it came to cancer I knew I had a choice. It could be an empowering experience or a disempowering one. I chose empowering. Sometimes it was as simple as saying *No* to a coffee date that I wasn't able for, but I had also tolerated inconsiderate and emotionally abusive behavior. It was a sure sign of low self-esteem that had dogged me all my life. Those relationships just disappeared. I cannot really explain what happened other than to say that I gradually started to feel an improved sense of self-worth. As I did, I could no longer tolerate being in environments where I was left feeling depleted or disrespected. At its most extreme, I would start to feel physically sick. My body was protecting me when I wasn't yet strong enough to assert healthy boundaries. Now it isn't an issue anymore. I genuinely have no interest and I realize, no responsibility, to be in situations which bring me down. I have worked too hard on myself and finally feel a sense of contentment that I am not willing to give away under any circumstance. I'm not saying that I won't be there to support and uplift others in their time of need. I absolutely will, more than I ever did, once my boundaries are respected and I am feeling well enough to do so.

Through no great foresight or planning of my own, I ended up doing two great courses with fabulous women. On the invitation of a friend, I attended a Louise Hay workshop run by a local woman Una Mc Nerney. I had always been an admirer of Louise Hay's work and had read her books – *You Can Heal Your Life* and *Heal Your Body*. She was a powerhouse of a woman who overcame great trauma. I loved how she talked about different approaches to life that I had never heard of. What started as a once-off workshop turned into more regular meetings and gave me a new lease of life. I connected with a group of like-minded women. We were all on our own paths of self-discovery and I felt honored to hear each of their stories and dreams. A few months after finishing treatment I was told about a course that is based on *The Artist's Way* book by Julia Cameron. It was such a gift and has been like a road map in my recovery. At first I thought – *This isn't for me. I'm not an artist.* I soon learnt that it isn't necessarily about becoming an artist. It is a spiritual program to help us to reconnect with the creative part of ourselves and to express this in whatever way feels right for us. The course, called *The Creative Life*, was developed by an extraordinary woman, Margie Connolly, and I felt at home the minute I stepped inside the door of her house. She lives in a beautiful, tranquil setting overlooking Galway Bay and straight away I knew that I was in a safe space where I could totally be myself. Confidences were shared, hopes expressed and trust developed as the weeks passed. There was lots of laughter too and cups of tea as the setting sun cast its warm glow over our little group. We worked our way through the course over six weeks and three years later we continue to meet on a monthly basis. Starting the course I had no creative outlet in my life and it really registered with me. Over coffee one morning, Margie asked me if I had ever thought about writing, which I hadn't. As I left her house I was totally unaware that her words had triggered something in me. That afternoon I felt drawn to my laptop and I started to write. I stayed writing for six months. The end result a few years later is this book. Life was definitely doing its best to help me. At every turn I was surrounded by the right people. There was no need for pretence. Most importantly, in both of these groups I met people who I gelled with very easily. When I spoke I felt seen and understood. These people got me!

I would encourage anyone facing a cancer diagnosis to reach out for support before starting treatment. It is hard to find the energy when you are overwhelmed with side effects and feeling low. I had experienced this during difficult times earlier in my life and I had withdrawn and isolated myself. I found it impossible to ask for help and believed nobody could understand how I felt. I was afraid to show my vulnerability. Now I was ready. I had the desire to get support and it was there. Everything just fell into place from the start. I cannot overstate the comfort and reassurance that comes from talking to others who have gone through a similar experience or are on their own path of growth and learning. Great strength comes from walking the path with like-minded people.

Gift

I was introduced to so many new people and got wonderful support. Never in my life had I felt so well looked after and cared for. I was being taught how to reach out and ask for help. I was also learning how to receive it. Now that I was ready I was looked after at every turn.

Chapter 10

Finding Balance

No one can listen to your body for you... To grow and heal, you have to take responsibility for listening to it yourself.
Jon Kabat-Zinn

As treatment finally ended, I felt relieved but mostly exhausted. I was also a little apprehensive about what lay ahead. I knew deep down that I couldn't, and didn't want to go back to the old life I had been living. It was time to not just start a new chapter but to write a new story for my life. I had just finished twenty-five daily sessions of radiotherapy. Each session takes about ten minutes, and as easy as it first appeared, I found the fatigue which accompanied it very debilitating. I suppose there was a cumulative effect from the chemotherapy and surgery, and I was reminded that my body was exhausted before I ever started treatment. I was determined to live a very different life, impatient almost, except I didn't have the energy to get moving.

I was scheduled to see my employer's occupational physician and felt nervous about what might be expected of me. It was a needless concern as they were so supportive. I just felt lost as I was no longer part of the medical system that had taken such good care of me. I couldn't believe that having gone through such a life-changing illness, there might be a presumption that I would slot back into my old life as if nothing had happened. It is understandable that once treatment is over, the doctors move on to the next patient needing attention. I found it a really difficult time emotionally which I hadn't expected. I felt totally off balance and didn't know how to get back on solid ground. Nothing prepares you for the aftermath. After all the efforts to rid your body of cancer, you are literally abandoned and left to your own devices. It is difficult for others to understand that the old you who got cancer doesn't exist anymore. A whole new person is emerging. This person thinks differently, feels different, has different values, dreams and a perspective on life that they never had. I would challenge anyone who has had a life-threatening illness to say it didn't change them at their core. You can't have a brush with your mortality without it leaving some impression. I know that we all process it in our own way and find different means of coping; for some that may mean returning to their old life, for others it may mean forging a new life that has more meaning and fulfillment. I was in the latter category. There is always a choice. If we truly want to change our lives, trust me it is possible. The unknown was a terrifying prospect for me back then. Now I try to embrace it, as I know it's where the magic of creation happens.

I had expected that I would have my energy back within a couple of months and I felt an urgency to take steps in a new direction. For quite a while I felt a strained tension between the past and a possible future and I was hanging in limbo. I had to get comfortable living with a lot of uncertainty and it was a big challenge for me. I felt I was up against the clock as I endeavored to build a new life. Fatigue continued to keep me in check and hampered any progress that I tried to make. It took me time to give in and go with it. For anyone who has experienced fatigue, they will know it is nothing like the tiredness you get from everyday living. I had plenty of experience of that. I had a busy day job that also involved working at evening events or driving the country late at night. Now here I was hitting a wall both mentally and physically just after meeting a friend for coffee or going to the shop. I felt like a shadow of my former self. There were no reserves left to dig into. Many times I just wanted to cry from how overwhelmed and vulnerable I felt. I didn't have the energy to explain and there really isn't any point. It is impossible for anyone who hasn't gone through something similar, through no fault of their own, to really understand what it feels like. I got a few sharp reminders of my old life, lest I forget. Two particular encounters really brought this home to me. In a shop one day I got chatting to the owner. I had been a regular there before I got sick. Our conversation turned to cancer and out of the blue she said – *You were always rushing when you came in here and looked like you were under a lot of pressure. You seem so different and relaxed now.* I was stopped in my tracks and memories of the old me came flooding back. Not long after that I had an appointment with my counselor and she too commented on how different I seemed – *I always knew you were on your way. I'd hear you running down the alleyway. You were always running.* These are only two small incidents. I could recount many more. This was how I lived my life. Full on-autopilot! I kept running as I was afraid of stopping. Funny, it was the people who didn't see me regularly who pointed out the change. Maybe I just found it easier to be more open with those who didn't know me so well.

As the weeks turned into months, my life started to take on an easy rhythm. I stopped pushing myself and felt new compassion for my body. I had been through a lot and I needed the time to rest and recuperate. I didn't feel as worried about doctors' appointments anymore as I was being honest about how I felt. I knew what my body needed. I was learning to live with uncertainty and be okay with it; to trust life. I had never been good at that. Something much more powerful took over and I was happy to let go. Everything I needed just happened without any great effort, and at the right time. I realized that the struggles I had experienced in the past were not because of the circumstances of my life or other people. There had been conflict between the life I was living and the life that I felt called to live. I had to be removed from it to gain perspective. I was also a people-pleaser and craved the approval of others. I learnt that I couldn't look to others for validation. This was an inner job that only I could do. I became more present in my life, with people, and with the uncertainty. Because I was open to it, synchronicity showed up at every turn – advice just when I needed it, recurring thoughts, chance meetings, strong instincts or urges to do something. The difference was, now I was really paying attention. I had quieted down inside and felt connected with a higher aspect of myself. I developed a sense of knowing. I was in touch with my intuition. The best decisions and actions in my life have always come from there. It is that wise voice inside all of us. Albert Einstein's words sum it up best for me – *The intuitive mind is a sacred gift and the rational mind is a faithful servant. We have created a society that honors the servant and has forgotten the gift.* I heard about a Cancer Rehabilitation Program in a new clinic in Galway and that was a life-saver. In my daily life I met people who have turned out to be great mentors and friends. I got recommendations for courses that were right up my alley and words of encouragement from unexpected encounters. Everything started to fall into place. In case I'm sounding like I just sat back and did nothing, it was actually quite the opposite. The key was that rather than overthinking, I let my intuition guide me and then employed my mind to work in my favor. I had a focus and I acted on what would move me in the right direction rather than mindless activity that wasn't serving a clear purpose. As I was finding balance and harmony in my life, I got a very clear vision of who I was and a direction for my life followed quite naturally. As hard as it can be to accept, times of great loss or devastation can be opportunities for great growth and healing. I know that from personal experience. It is only we who can choose how we respond. I now had an opportunity to change the course of my life or just step back into my old one. I have no doubt that if I had chosen the latter I would be telling you a different story a few years from now. Likely it would be a story of some other illness or crisis that had occurred to wake me up. I just knew that something had to change. Now I feel a sense of purpose and I am determined to follow it. I had never found the business of living very easy. Nonetheless, my struggles taught me life skills, skills that I can now use to support others who are ready to choose a path of growth. They also gave me a strength that I could call on later in life. It was part of a bigger plan. I now see my purpose as a way of being in every moment, not a destination. It was time to follow my inner nudges, not what I believed were others' expectations of me. To me that is true freedom. It is all still work in progress and I have to make a conscious effort not to overdo it and start running again at a mile a minute. Old habits die hard, but I have no interest in the rat race nor am I able for it anymore. I know I always have a choice. I have never been driven by material success just for its own sake as I know it is not a ticket to happiness. It is just a nice by-product of living my life well. The excesses of the Celtic Tiger period in Ireland are proof of that. The tragic suicides, during the recession that followed surely point to a shaky sense of self-worth that was measured only in terms of material success. I now trust that if I follow my true calling, I will always be supported. I will have enough. It may not be in the way that our materialistic world tells me I should be supported, but that is only a vicious circle that never satisfies. Arianna Huffington, co-founder of the *Huffington Post*, wrote her book *Thrive* on this very topic. She shares her own wake-up call in life. She collapsed from exhaustion, while running a hugely successful business:

> *In terms of traditional measures of success, which focus on money and power, I was very successful. But I was not living a successful life by any sane definition of success. I knew something had to radically change. I could not go on that way.*

She goes on to describe what she sees as another important

metric of a successful life, consisting of 4 pillars – well-being, wisdom, wonder and giving. I came upon it at just the right time, when I was drawn to reading books on the subject of consciousness and transformation. They were exactly what I needed and as I had been given the time, I wanted to use it wisely, nourishing my soul and exploring answers to the bigger questions in life. It is still the case today. I also learnt another valuable lesson. There is a big difference between giving your energy to something you love versus doing something you don't feel fulfilled by. In the words of motivational speaker Simon Sinek – *Working hard for something we don't care about is called stress; working hard for something we love is called passion.* Somewhere along the way, my passion and enthusiasm had been replaced by stress and my body was mirroring it back to me. The sands had shifted. I had enjoyed a great career in sales and marketing for twenty-five years, but in the end I felt burnt out. I had a strong desire to expand and work in a more holistic way. I was also lonely for a connection with like-minded people. I felt that I wasn't expressing who I truly was. Life is not static. It is constantly in motion. When the time is right it prods us to move on and evolve. When we resist we suffer. I was learning to let go and move on. Whatever you do – run a business, look after your children, work in a coffee shop – it doesn't matter as long as it is nourishing you in some way. It is the common denominator in the contented people that I have met, whatever their level of material success. When we move with life as opposed to fighting it, everything gets easier. I was learning about balance too. As it was explained to me, you can't keep making withdrawals from your bank of energy without making some deposits. Eventually the bank runs dry and stress, illness or some other crisis is the end result. I'm living proof of that! In the words of author and internationally-renowned speaker, Caroline Myss, *What drains your spirit drains your body. What fuels your spirit fuels your body.*

Gift

Fatigue turned out to be a great gift. Though I felt very frustrated and overwhelmed at times, it was nature's way of slowing me down and helping me get back on track. I have no doubt that if I had bounced back quickly from cancer, I wouldn't have had the time to truly get the lessons of my illness and move forward in a purposeful way.

Chapter 11

Coming Back To Life

When we experience the loss of our outer life, the way to our inner light is cleared.
Heidi DuPree

As time passed, I felt like I was being brought back to life through my cancer experience. My hard drive had been wiped clean and I was being rebooted with an upgrade. That is the simplest way to describe how radically different I felt. If you are facing your own struggles, my words might be hard to relate to right now, yet for others they may ring true. I just share what honestly has been my experience in the hope that it will help anyone who is going through a difficult time. There is light at the end of a challenging period although it isn't always easy to see when you're going through it. Think back to other dark times in your life. You came out the other side. You are much more powerful and resilient than you likely give yourself credit for. There were many books I read and words that resonated with me. All deeply touched me and were instrumental in changing how I looked at life. I was ready. I started to feel something stirring deep inside. The higher calling that I mentioned in Chapter 1 was starting to make itself known. I suppose the truth is that I had been feeling quite dead inside for some time. I found it hard to get excited or passionate about anything. Life felt monotonous and mechanical. While driving to work, I had often thought – *This can't be it*. I couldn't believe that the main reason I was here on earth was just to exist and pay bills. My life had to have more meaning than that. I had to have some greater purpose. I had met many people living a life they loved, but I also heard others talk about what they couldn't do because of responsibilities or fear. I wanted to be in the first camp. If having a mortgage or bills was going to stop me from living a fulfilling life and following my dreams, something was definitely very wrong. I didn't want my legacy to be – *She paid her mortgage off*. They are not mutually exclusive. I didn't have children or that kind of family life. It had taken time, but I had come to terms with it. For many, that makes everything they do worthwhile. They have a clear purpose and it gives their life meaning. That wasn't me. I felt a strong impulse to understand what made me tick. I needed my life to be about making a difference in the world, even in some small way. Most importantly, I had an ache inside to feel passion for my life, to expand and really feel alive.

I recognized that making change wasn't just about what I did for a living although my work is an integral part of my life. I am at my best when there is meaning and purpose to my work and it reflects who I am and what is important to me. I think that goes for everyone, yet deep down we often don't believe it is possible. I now know that it is, if I'm willing to change my perspective. I started to see that change was also about how I lived my life every day; my beliefs, attitude, actions, relationships, every aspect of my life. It really did take losing everything connected with my former life for me to understand that. It happened gradually with lots of little *ah ha* moments along the way. It was like the intelligence of the universe was slowly revealing itself to me in a way that I could understand, without being overwhelmed. It was taking me by the hand and gently leading me into a new future.

I don't believe there are any accidents or coincidences in life. In fact, in mathematics, the term coincident refers to something that fits perfectly. To me, this is how the universe works. Everything we see in our outer world is just a reflection of our inner world. As I recognized this, everything started to make sense. Like an intricate picture, it is only on close examination that we see things not apparent at first glance. Our perception of it changes. So too with life. We can never see the full picture of a person or situation, we can, however, be open to looking deeper or choosing a different view. It took a lot of honesty and willingness for me to accept the truth. It wasn't about blame. It was just part of the process of life and inevitable growth that we all face at one point or another. I could choose to be a victim of circumstance and a spectator in my life, or I could choose to be an active participant and co-creator of my life. I knew enough to know that I couldn't go backwards. I couldn't unsee what I had seen or unknow what I now knew. As a result, new opportunities and possibilities started to appear. Cancer was giving me an opportunity to start afresh and I didn't want to waste it. In fact I was hungry for it and I could see a new path opening up in front of me. My thoughts and feelings about my future were starting to create my reality. I can't say this enough. It was key. Once I was able to visualize what it might look like, feel it and focus on it, it couldn't but start to unfold. I needed help and guidance to get to this place, but the answers came from inside. I suppose this was the biggest change. I started to view my life differently. I was shifting from being a victim of life to living from a place of authentic power. I now describe it as life happening *for* me, not *to* me. It was a radical shift in perspective and I look at life through that lens to this day. As difficult as it can be sometimes, I do my best to see challenges as learning moments and opportunities for growth. I cannot adequately express how holding this perspective has absolutely transformed my experience of life. It really is a miracle.

Around this time, I came across a TedTalk by an American woman called Victoria Labalme, a coach and performing artist. She also trained as a mime artist with Marcel Marceau in France and brings these techniques to her work in a really unique way. The talk is called, *Risk Forward: The Rewards of Not Knowing*. Something clicked inside when I watched it. It was particularly relevant to me at the time as I was stepping into a new and unknown future. For anyone who is in transition and unclear about their goals or direction, she explains it as a philosophy for moving forward in times of uncertainty. She describes the inner current or *through line* in our lives. This is a theatre term, coined by the Russian Theatre artist Stanislavski, to describe the driving force in a character's behavior. We can adapt this idea to our lives. What is driving us through our life? What is our *through line*? When we trust it and take a step forward, we can see things we didn't see before we took that step. Our *through line* leads us to the next right step where we can see new possibilities. We don't have to have all the answers, in fact it is impossible. We just need to take a step in the right direction and trust. I would highly recommend watching this TedTalk, particularly if you're at a time of transition in your life. It helped me move forward, step by step, and eased any anxiety about what might lie ahead. At the same time, it didn't come naturally to me. I often took one step forward and then two steps back. There were times when it felt like the whole world was against me and I would be better off just going back to my old life. Much of that was in my head. My inner critic was alive and well! I learnt that change happens gradually and sometimes we have to revisit old territory and make sure we have learnt the lessons before we move forward again. I had many wobbly moments and still do. Now I don't see them as the end of the world. I choose to look at them as little tests to make sure I'm on the right track and not going too fast. Change doesn't always happen at the pace we believe it should. Time is often needed to fully integrate and process all that is happening. I know there is a divine timing at play in my life and I now trust it to decide when I am ready on all levels.

I started to feel a new respect and appreciation for my life. I felt like I was coming home to myself. For the first time ever I felt worthy. I was surprised by how much I enjoyed my own company. *The Creative Life* course was the start of a new passion unfolding for me. I found that I loved writing and needed it. It has made a phenomenal difference to me and has awoken a much-needed avenue for self-expression. I was finding my voice and getting comfortable with it. I felt very drawn to work that is about healing, transformation and positive change. This led me to train as a life coach. I was proud of how far I had come and the work I had done to overcome personal challenges. I was starting to feel that I had something to offer the world. I was stepping into my personal power and I wanted to help others do the same. I truly believe that we all have the capacity for greatness in our lives. We are not here to fit in. We are here to stand out. We are here to be distinctive and embrace what makes us unique. My passion is to support others who want to do what I have been helped to do, to heal what is holding them back so that they can bring their gifts to life. I knew I was on the right track when I felt energized, excited and passionate about what I was doing. I listened to the higher aspect of myself, my *through line*. We might choose different ways to access that core part of ourselves. It could be meditation for some, being in nature for others. I see it as anything that slows me down and allows me to cultivate a sense of inner space. I found Wayne Dyer's *Getting in the Gap* meditation really helpful. The gap refers to the gap between our thoughts. In his words:

> *It's the silence between the notes that makes the music – is an ancient Zen observation, which clarifies this idea. Imagine, if you can, music without pauses or silent spaces. Without the pauses for silence, the music would be one infinitely long note of noise. What we call music would be impossible. This is true for all of creation, including the world that you wish to create for yourself. Creativity itself is a function of the gap.*

It took me time to readjust to the world that I had been absent from. I found it hard to relate to the speed and pace of life. I met so many people running through their lives and I was no longer able to keep up. Enquiries as to someone's welfare were nearly always met with the answer – *busy*. It sounded like a strange badge of honor in a world that was already dealing with unprecedented levels of anxiety, depression and disconnection. I had never questioned my own way of living, because I too was busy being busy. It is not easy to slow down when all around you is speed. I believe we would be living in a slower, more connected type of world if we knew that we are enough just as we are. We would be happier. There is nothing to prove. Maybe it is time for that now. I know there are many demands on everyone, yet we always have a choice to say *No*. I learnt that one the hard way. What would it be like to totally unplug? To schedule in even half an hour to daydream or just let your mind wander. It is in the quiet that our true priorities start to make themselves known. I'll finish this chapter on a thought-provoking question that Victoria Labalme puts to the audience in her TedTalk:

If you were on a desert island and dying, and there was a young person there with you, someone you cared deeply about, and you could only give one piece of advice to that person before you died, a piece of advice about life, what would that advice be?

Whatever comes into your heart or mind is exactly right for you. It's what you believe really matters, that at the end of life, for you that's what it's really all about. So the challenge becomes – how can we bring that into our lives on a daily basis, to express that through line and risk forward to trust it with our own creative ideas to express it?

Gift

I was being shown a new, possible life that some part of me had always intended to live, but I had got lost along the way. Cancer helped me rediscover it. I will always be grateful for that.

Part II – Transformation

In this part of the book I cover the journey of integrating everything that I was learning from my illness and the impact it had on my life. As I recovered and moved around in the world again, I could see that the lessons were supporting me in everyday living and that I will never stop growing. There is no particular order to the chapters. I have just written them as they arose and as my understanding of life was changing. They reflect what I needed to learn and put into practice at the time, and still do. Writing has helped me process all that has happened. It keeps me focused and supports me in a new way of being.

Chapter 12

Appreciation

We tend to forget that happiness doesn't come as a result of getting something we don't have, but rather of recognizing and appreciating what we do have.
Friedrich Koenig

Appreciation or gratitude weren't ever high up on my list of priorities. I was grateful for a gift, some good news or a kind gesture, but I tended to focus on what I perceived as missing from my life. I looked at others and imagined them to be more fortunate than me. Although it wasn't a constant preoccupation, it was still enough to keep an undercurrent of dissatisfaction and frustration alive. Conversations I had with friends and colleagues were often a litany of complaints about others and the injustices in our lives. Even though I was a voluntary participant, I found it very draining and knew this wasn't a healthy way to live. It wasn't who I had been earlier in life. This was a new and exhausting experience and I got lost in it for quite a while. It seems a huge leap from then to now. I truly see my cancer as a gift and I appreciate what it has taught me and is still teaching me to this day. I don't think anything else could have stopped me in my tracks so completely. It gave me time to reassess my life and plot a new path. Although the car accident had hit the pause button for a while, it wasn't long before I was back on the hamster wheel at full speed. I was at a loss to know what to do and I was feeling very disillusioned with how my life had turned out.

So what changed? I got cancer and I recovered. I could just as easily have ended up back where I had been, still frustrated and feeling like a helpless spectator in my own life. A number of factors came into play. Fatigue played a role. I didn't have the energy to return to my old pace of life. Also, everything I read, watched, researched and was experiencing, pointed to the benefits of living with gratitude. Initially, it felt a bit clichéd and I doubted that feeling grateful could have any real life-changing impact on me. I knew it was an admirable quality. I just didn't see it as a state; that you could live in a state of gratitude or appreciation. I discovered that you can. It does take a shift in focus and a concerted effort to see life from a totally different perspective, at least initially. When I choose gratitude in any situation, it totally changes how I experience it. I know it isn't always easy to feel grateful, particularly if you feel that life has let you down or been unfair. I was rowing that boat for a long time. However, if you choose to see life like I now do, as an experience that we chose to have on earth, then it becomes a different playing field. Yes, difficult times come to us all. Even though we might not understand why, they are there to help us grow and expand. Ultimately it is our choice to stay stuck or evolve. I can't say that I would welcome going through my marriage breakdown again, I don't think I would be able, yet I honestly appreciate everything I learnt as a result. Kahlil Gibran in his poem "On Pain" tells us that, *Your pain is the breaking of the shell that encloses your understanding.* He explains that we would learn nothing about life if we didn't have struggles. Experiencing difficult times has definitely given my life a richness and depth that it couldn't have if it had just been plain sailing all the time. The true nature of life is duality, the experiencing of contrast – good and bad, happy and sad, light and day. How can you be truly happy or know what happiness is, if you have never experienced the opposite? Chinese philosopher, Lao Tzu explores this theme in his sacred text, *The Tao Te Ching.* It roughly translates as *The Way of Integrity* and was written more than two thousand years ago. It is regarded by many as the ultimate commentary on the nature of existence.

In the second verse he says – *Under heaven all can see beauty as beauty; only because there is ugliness.* Opposites are necessary for the experiencing of life.

I feel a great sense of contentment today and I know it is because of all that I have experienced. I have discovered depths of strength that I had no idea I possessed. Facing our fears really does open us up to the possibility of great joy and freedom. There really is nothing to fear. It is just the projections of our mind and our belief in them. A belief is just a thought repeated and we have the power to choose a different thought in any moment. Understanding this has been truly liberating, even if it is not always easy to put into practice.

Another breakthrough was accepting that I have no control over how life plays out. I can only control how I respond to it. I knew this in theory, yet I still lived in a way that was attached to the need for control. I felt very let down when things didn't go my way. I caused myself endless amounts of suffering by not accepting the reality of life as it was. No gratitude in that attitude. I often avoided difficult conversations or standing up for myself. I was a people pleaser, and I didn't just want to be liked, I needed to be liked. I thought that if I behaved in a certain way, I would get the external validation that I had always craved, a futile endeavor. I often dishonored myself in the process or went against my better judgment and just ended up feeling worse. I couldn't control having cancer, so I had to learn to let go and focus on all that I had to be grateful for. Learning to trust life and work with what unfolds has been my biggest lesson to date. It was Michael A. Singer's book, *The Surrender Experiment,* that really brought it home to me.

As I write, I use the words gratitude and appreciation interchangeably, yet I do think there is a subtle difference between them. To me gratitude is about receiving something. Appreciation, however, is not based on getting something necessarily; it is about recognizing all that we have to be thankful for already. It can take a crisis or a rock bottom for that to happen. That was definitely true for me. The gift of life took on a whole new meaning after my diagnosis with cancer. It was around this time that I was first introduced to a spiritual teacher called Mooji. I felt a great internal shift when I started following his teachings. I haven't felt the same since. As I started to follow his guidance and connect with my inner world, I began to have moments of great peace. No money, job or material possession could match it in any way. When I started to feel more appreciative it seemed like miracles showed up every day. That is no exaggeration. I felt so happy, and still do, sometimes from the simplest things. I might just be walking by the sea or doing nothing in particular and I find myself smiling. I mentioned that old and new friends rallied round and I was never short of a kind word, encouragement or support. I can't count the cups of coffee and lunches I had, and to this day I appreciate every single one of them. The encounters were always genuine and coming from the heart. There is nothing more nurturing, in my book. One particular friend, Caroline, who I had only known for a few years and primarily on a professional basis through work, was my life raft in the early days. She checked in on me almost daily, sent me lovely thoughtful messages and listened when I was feeling overwhelmed or worried about my future. I didn't have to pretend to be okay with her and that was such a relief.

My ex-husband Brian reappeared in my life. He had gone through his own experience of losing a sister to cancer and another sister surviving breast cancer. When we first met through work many years before, the connection was instant. I have a crystal clear memory of my first encounter with him and the contagious sound of his laughter from across the office. Something in me recognized him and once we were introduced I felt like I had known him forever. We gelled easily and it wasn't long before we were spending a lot of time together. Our relationship developed naturally and we got married in 1999. Sadly the marriage came to an end after three years, but that is another story for another time. The breakup was unavoidable and very traumatic for both of us. Although no one was at fault, it was still no insulation against the onslaught of pain that accompanied the split. We had little contact for the first few years as it was just too hard. We both needed time to heal and find our own way in life. We checked in with each other sporadically after the years had passed, but we were living different lives by then. Ironically it was my diagnosis with cancer which brought us back into each other's lives and in a deeper way. The love between us had never died and it only proved to me how strong the bond between us is. Time and trauma hadn't dimmed it. We are now very close friends. It is a soul mate relationship for sure and one I treasure very much. Once Brian heard my news, he started to visit me regularly while I was going through treatment. I really looked forward to his visits. We always spent our time deep in conversation and laughing a lot like we used to. It seemed to be just the right time to reconnect. We had both struggled to find our way after splitting up. We were only thirty-four and had to go about rebuilding our lives from scratch. That hadn't been an easy task for either of us. We had each experienced dark times which ultimately led us down paths of great growth and development. Each time we met I was reminded of the shared passion and enthusiasm we had once shared for life. It encouraged me to pick myself up after cancer and follow my heart no matter what the seeming obstacles. We are now an integral part of each other's lives and I am beyond grateful for that.

I also came to appreciate my family more, particularly my mother. As I recovered after surgery, she took very good care of me and has supported me every step of the way since. I have spent a lot of time with her and I will always be grateful for it. I wouldn't be doing what I'm doing now if it wasn't for her unconditional, loving presence in my life. I reconnected with old friends too in a deeper way. My great friend, Rachel, whom I met on my first day at work in 1990, has always been, and continues to be, a steadfast and inspiring influence in my life. I made wonderful new friends and this tribe continues to spur me on to follow my dreams. I rediscovered the value of community, connection and good neighbors. I felt anchored in my life. I put down roots again, roots that gave me the courage to fly high and dream big.

Finally, the most important thing I discovered is that real happiness doesn't come from getting all the *things* I thought would make me happy. It only cements in the feeling that something is missing when I am always looking to the external world to satisfy me. I realized that life is made up of a series of moments and if I didn't start appreciating them, it would quickly pass me by. Through the ups and downs, I try my best now to pay attention and be present. None of us escape pain or devastation. We can, however, choose our attitude. I started a practice of writing in a gratitude journal. I don't necessarily do it every day. Sometimes I just take a moment to focus on feeling grateful, particularly if my day didn't go as planned. It can totally shift my perspective. I know that if I don't genuinely feel grateful it is just an empty exercise. It is definitely a truth that you can't feel stressed and grateful at the same time. It's just not possible.

Gift

Life – I started to appreciate it. We never know when the end is coming. I needed the jolt of cancer to wake me up to the realization that all I have is the here and now. That is all any of us have. I don't want to sound morbid, but I hold no fear of death anymore. If it were to arrive tomorrow I would be okay with that because I have remembered who I am and why I am here.

Chapter 13

Being Present With What Is

The ability to be in the present moment is a major component of mental wellness.
Abraham Maslow

This has been one of my greatest challenges and something I still have to pay attention to. Throughout my life, I often found it hard to stay present, with myself or others. When alone, I had to keep busy. I needed constant distraction, so I was always doing something. The idea of just being, seemed impossible. It was a luxury that I shouldn't indulge in our fast-paced world. Similarly, when in the company of others, I was often lost in thought and the stories going on in my head. I may have been there in body and felt I was listening, but I didn't really know what being present meant. Now I see it as being conscious and open in the moment, whatever is going on. Cancer showed me this. My life became a lot quieter when I started treatment and I surrendered to it. I needed it. As I emerged into the world afterwards, it would have been very easy for me to revert to old ways, but something had changed. I just knew that the present moment was the only place that I could fully experience life and I was determined to do the work to help me settle there.

Old traumas or painful emotions can be at the root of our difficulty to just *be* in the moment. The fear of them resurfacing keeps us on the move, both mentally and physically, so that we don't have to face them. That was the case for me. It is just part and parcel of the human journey that we will all experience trauma. It could be unhealthy ancestral patterns passed down through the generations or it may be the result of a very difficult experience, like a physical attack or abuse. It can also be the result of an event that appears quite benign on the surface, particularly as a child. It could be a harsh word, getting lost, being excluded, not being seen – basically our needs not being met. It may be unconscious on the part of others but it can leave scars that stay with us and build inside if the experience is repeated. We may have let ourselves be open, vulnerable, expecting love and it wasn't there for us. We are afraid to be present in case we get stuck in the pain or are hurt again. After my marriage ended I developed a reflex action if I felt anyone was getting too close. I detached and kept them at a distance. I was a bit of a lone wolf and although I had a good social circle, there were few people I really let in. Exploring our wounds is not about dredging up the past or assigning blame. It is about taking responsibility and clearing out the heavy emotional residue that can otherwise hold us back. We drop our baggage and heal the pain. I had to do it, and I'm so glad that I did. Life then becomes an experience that we enjoy and can handle no matter what is going on. Although I still face difficult situations, I feel a great capacity to stay afloat no matter what life throws at me.

The end of my marriage in 2002 was extremely painful. It triggered feelings of depression which I didn't realize at the time. I felt devastated and worthless. Low self-esteem had always been with me to some extent and it reached an all-time low at that time. I felt very alone and unable to process what had happened. I thought there must something very wrong with me. As I scrambled to survive I took a holiday with a friend to the island of Zakynthos in Greece. While there I met a Greek man and dived headlong into a relationship that was a welcome reprieve from how I felt. The holiday fling quickly turned into a year-long hiatus from my old life, a life that I couldn't bear to return to. When I came back to Ireland, I applied for a career break. I trained as a TEFL teacher and returned to Greece, this time to the town of Patras on the mainland, where he lived.

I would have done anything to escape what I saw as my car crash of a life. I had some good times in Greece. The scenery was breathtaking and the weather glorious. I got a job teaching English in the mornings and the afternoons were usually spent on the beach. I know, it sounds idyllic. It looked like one long summer holiday from the outside, but that wasn't the reality. I was extremely lonely and I hadn't even started to come to terms with the fact that my life had fallen apart. I was a stranger in a city where English was rarely if ever spoken and I had little Greek. I had moved country to live with someone I hardly knew, so it wasn't surprising that it came to an end within the year. I was left with the prospect of picking up the pieces of my life when I moved back home to Galway and that wasn't easy. Although I might have appeared to be functioning, I wasn't functioning in a healthy way. I couldn't shake the constant feelings of emptiness and depression that only intensified with my return. The life that I had spent many years building in Dublin was nonexistent and it was terrifying. I worked hard and used alcohol to block out the pain. It was the only coping mechanism I knew. I have no qualms admitting that I had many dark nights of the soul where I hoped that I wouldn't wake up the next day. I am grateful that I didn't actively plan suicide although I came very close. I felt huge pain and I had no idea how to articulate the extent of it. It was very isolating. I only got to that point a few years after my marriage broke down, so if I had actually taken the step, I think very few people would have understood why. Eventually I got help and turned things around. Extreme life events kickstarted a journey of soul-searching and self-discovery and it is a journey that continues to this day. Even though I didn't realize it at the time, I was only starting out and there were many more life lessons yet to come.

My interest in natural approaches to health led me to study craniosacral therapy in 2013. I wanted to learn more about the mind-body connection. During the course we covered a module called somato-emotional release (SER). The word soma is a Greek word meaning body. Old traumas or negative emotional experiences are held in our body in the form of energy cysts (blocked energy) and keep us stuck. That made total sense to me. What manifests as a physical problem can usually be traced back to the origins of an old story in our life. As was often said on the course, the issues are in the tissues. During the training we carried out a number of SER sessions on our fellow students. It is a very gentle therapy combining bodywork and dialogue with the client. During these sessions everyone experienced the release of some old trauma they were still holding on to. The impact was astounding. I witnessed people relive old experiences and have huge, cathartic emotional releases. I returned to the experience of having my tonsils and adenoids removed in hospital when I was two years old. Panic came up and it felt as real as if it were happening in real time, even though I have no clear memory of it. My mother also told me that I suffered with night terrors after coming out of hospital. Although we move on, the memory of difficult past experiences are stored in our body and we function more healthily when they are released. Sometimes we have irrational fears and phobias and we have no idea why – the body knows why. It really brought home to me that being present with whatever is going on in life, good or bad, is a powerful way to be. It is how we come through an experience and grow. We don't get to bypass difficult experiences. We might shut down and become depressed or end up in a cycle of suffering and anxiety. Whatever we do, the emotions always resurface at a later stage. I could have won many medals for my efforts at running away. Pema Chödrön's book *The Places That Scare You* explores this topic. She tells us that coming to grips with pain and discomfort is the key to growth encouraging ... *stay present to the pain of disapproval or betrayal...* She suggests that when we do this it softens us. Otherwise we just become very brittle. Chödrön says that it is actually a relief when we let ourselves feel the intensity of a feeling. I can vouch for that 100%. Suppressing painful feelings had only left me feeling depressed and in despair. They are guaranteed to bring us down eventually.

My car accident in 2014 was another reminder to slow down. I was feeling overwhelmed generally and on some level I was glad of the distraction of work. I travelled all over the country, visiting schools and attending events, the more the better. Yet inside I felt empty. I also had a number of very draining relationships in my life and I didn't know where to turn. Around that time I was told of a healer called Pádraig who lived nearby in the countryside. Although I wasn't really sure why I was going to him, I felt like I was going to explode if I didn't do something. I drove out to his house and was met by a very gentle, unassuming man who made me feel at ease as soon as I walked in the door. I spent almost three hours with him. During the session, he cupped my head with his hands while I just lay there. We spoke little apart from a few words when he explained what he was sensing. I can't recall much of what took place. I just know that I left feeling calm and physically very tired. It was a few days later while on my way to an exercise class that I started to feel nauseous. I was overcome by emotion and I started to cry uncontrollably as I sat in the car. I had no idea what was happening and couldn't stop. I had never experienced anything like it before. The exact same thing happened when I was at work the next day and I had to leave the office in a hurry. In desperation I rang Pádraig and asked for help. He reassured me that I would be okay. He said that I was ready to be free of old painful emotions and that a higher part of me had agreed to it at our session. That may sound strange, yet intuitively I already knew that was the case. At the same time it was frightening as there was no stopping this purging of emotions when I felt it coming on. He reassured me that I was strong enough to release them. I didn't need to know what they were about or to analyze them. He told me to ask that it happen when I was alone and could release privately, which I did. And from that day forward that is exactly what happened. I was never in the company of others when the urge would come over me. To me, that is a miracle. The only way I can describe the experience is to compare it to feeling really nauseous. I would drive to a car park and then spend however long it took to get it all out. It felt like it was rising from my feet, a tsunami of emotion that I was vomiting out. I felt exhausted afterwards but also on a high. This continued on and off for about a month, with the intensity dwindling as time went on. It isn't an overnight job when you have been suppressing uncomfortable feelings for years. It was a surreal experience, and a necessary one. It allowed me to move out of the past and become present in my life. It was such a huge relief to clear old, stagnant energy from my body. I could breathe again. That light, spacious feeling has never left me. It has only expanded since my experience with cancer.

Having come from a place of having no healthy coping skills, I was starting to feel empowered and capable of navigating life's challenges. This woke a burning desire in me to help others do the same for themselves. That is why I trained as a life coach. Being present took on new meaning as it is one of the key cornerstones in the coaching relationship – the ability to *dance in the moment* with a client. It requires a keen level of attention and presence to what is happening in the person. You are not planning ahead or working off a prepared script, instead you are responding to exactly how they show up. This is where the real magic happens as both client and coach are in the moment together. It is amazing the impact it has on another person when you risk being really present with them, not advising, just staying with them as they go wherever they need to go. They feel heard, understood and it is very empowering. Often after a coaching session, I might have felt that I didn't *do* very much, yet the client recounted how helpful it was to be really listened to and understood. They had space to explore and get in touch with their inner wisdom. When we are with someone who is essentially our cheerleader, we feel safe to be authentic and our best selves. It has a power that we often underestimate, a power that helps us move forward. That has definitely been the case for me.

When I spend a lot of time worrying about the future it also reminds me that I need to re-center. As I started to feel better after treatment, I immediately wanted a new life. I was afraid of going back to the past and I had no idea what lay ahead. I spent a lot of time worrying needlessly about everything – where I would live, how I would support myself financially, what work I would do, and on and on. It becomes an automatic way of being, always moving on to the next thing to worry about or desire. It is a vicious cycle where we rarely feel satisfied as we can never know what the future holds. That is living unconsciously, and when we live unconsciously we miss out on opportunities or synchronicities that are showing us the way. Now I see the present as the place that I heal and let go of the past, and where I consciously create my future. It is where I align with the energy of creation. If I am rarely there then life is just happening to me. Life experience has taught me how to be at peace with myself and how to process emotions healthily. It has been a tough life lesson, and one I won't forget; the only way through difficult emotions is *through*. There is no bypassing them. Suppressed emotions always come to the surface at some point, and in my case they ultimately manifested as dis-ease in the body. I have found *The Untethered Soul* by Michael A. Singer to be a great resource for living well and dealing with emotional upsets. Now when I feel discomfort or tension, I sit, breathe and set the intention to release them. I sit until I feel the energy physically move and it does. I also follow a diaphragmatic breathing practice which is a very powerful tool for moving energy. Releasing stuck emotions can be difficult initially as we have to feel them. It requires courage and a desire to be free, but it is so worth it. Emotions really are just energy in motion (e-motion) and they are meant to move through us. It is when we resist that they get lodged in us and we suffer terribly as a result. We end up with a body that is full of pent-up energy. We are like a fizzy drink with the lid screwed on tight. If we don't release the cap gradually and slowly, it will explode when we open it. Doing this at regular intervals prevents us from getting totally overwhelmed by life. American clinical psychologist, Peter A. Levine, has worked in the field of stress and trauma for over forty years. He developed the Somatic Experiencing® method. This is a body-oriented approach to the healing of trauma and stress disorders and it has been his life's work. He received his PhD in medical biophysics from the University of California in Berkeley and also holds a doctorate in psychology from International University. He has also written many books on the subject of trauma. He reminds us that all indigenous cultures have practices for releasing energy from the body. However, in the Western world we are trained to bypass our emotions, to appear normal and be productive members of society – neither healthy nor helpful. I am so grateful that I was directed on a path of healing and sent many people who were able to support me. Today I have great self-compassion and empathy for others who are suffering. It takes time, but when you come out the other side your life becomes transformed in unimaginable ways and you develop the skills to help yourself.

Once I healed old emotions I felt free to live in a way that nurtured me as a whole person. Nutrition, exercise and meeting people who lifted my spirits had a huge impact on my well-being. The single most important change that happened was my thirst to explore the spiritual side of my life. I think I always had an ache inside to live in a deeper way, yet I never knew how. The emptiness I felt had nothing to do with the external world, although I often found it easier to look to it to satisfy me. I find it difficult to write about this aspect of my life as it is very personal. It is also something each of us experiences in our own time. It is not an intellectual concept that we can learn. It is beyond the psychological mind and accessed only through the heart. It is a calling that comes from deep within when we are ready. All I can say is that the right people and right guidance came into my life at the right time. That led me to find Wayne Dyer, the teachings of Mooji, a great spiritual teacher who changed my life, along with the beautiful, Dr. Yvonne Murphy, and many more. New teachers continue to appear in my life at just the right time. I will finish this chapter with a short story told by Mooji. It gives a sense of what being present means to me. It really touched me when I first heard it. It is an extract from a book by Mooji, *Vaster Than Sky, Greater Than Space*, where he recounts a parable from the Bhagavad Gita, an important Hindu text.

It showed two birds in a tree, and one of them was building a nest. This one is flying off collecting things, arranging the twigs – it's active, doing many things. Above this bird on another branch, is a second bird. It looks identical to the first bird, but it's not building anything. It is just observing. It's not building a self-image out of its perceiving, and it's not deeply interested in any aspect of what it sees. Its perceiving is happening quite spontaneously without effort or judgment. There's a silence there, that feeling of being without thought. Just looking. This is a beautiful portrait of who we are. These two birds are connected. The first bird represents our dynamic being, the self that is engaged in the world, in future and past, in growing. It is the aspect that is living life with the sense of "my family, my children, my work, and so on." The second bird represents that conscious witnessing within us. It is the ability to observe life taking place and activities unfolding, but it is not actually doing anything. It is still within the same body, but it is not manipulating. It is not saying, "I hope this, and I fear that."

No, it is very still. It is simply there, and its seeing is panoramic. It sees not only the first bird, but also the wind in the trees, the sky – everything is observed with a kind of neutrality.

Initially the first bird is very identified with building the nest. It may not even be aware of the second bird. But as soon as it is able to be quiet, it becomes aware of the second bird, which is actually itself at a deeper inner level. When the first bird's mind is synchronized with the second bird, the activities become much more gracious.

There is a sense of unity, a oneness. In that harmony, the work may still happen but without obsession, without fear, without the sense of needing to control things. It is simply happening because life compels this activity to happen. It is as though another power is helping the actions to take place. The second bird represents the change of perspective from the mode of person to the state of presence. When we are involved in the activities of life so deeply that it seems that the daily routine is all there is, then we are like this first bird, the nest builder, oblivious to our second bird position.

Come to the second bird position, to the one who is observing, and you will discover that the one who is busy building a life will slowly become more transparent, leaving only the functioning itself. The activities are happening anyway, beautifully, but the sense of doer-ship – which is the ego sense – will fade away. Activities are just happening; our self-image as a person is just happening, but our true Self is not a happening. In fact, the true Self is a third position, which is not a bird, but the space within which both birds are arising and seen.

This story reminds me that there is a deeper place within, where I can rest, feel at peace and whole. It is a place beyond thought. It is my true self. As I now practice meditation on a daily basis, I'm settling into that place. It is a practice that has changed my life immeasurably. It doesn't have to be for long periods, but you need to persist. Soon you will want to keep coming back, because you know it is home. In time you will radiate the benefits out into the world. It has radically changed my experience of life and helped me become more present with myself and others.

Gift

I can only say that I am like a baby learning to walk as I endeavor to shift my perspective from the mode of person and busyness to the state of presence. Yet even at this early stage I have found a whole new world and an infinite sense of space inside. I feel less caught up in the day-to-day dramas of life. I can sit quite easily in my own company and I find time spent in the company of people I really connect with deeply enriching.

Chapter 14

Living Without Limits

There is one grand lie – that we are limited. The only limits we have are the limits we believe.
Wayne Dyer

Up until cancer knocked on my door, I lived quite a fearful life, seeing myself as small and so many things out of my reach. I looked at others who seemed to be living their dream and I would feel an ache inside. Only now can I see that I was dishonoring myself. I felt like I was suffocating long before I ever got sick. I was unhappy and struggled to pinpoint what was wrong. I just knew this couldn't be the way I was meant to live. I felt like I was suppressing who I really was and that my life force was dimming. I only started to believe that life was full of possibilities when I embarked on my training to be a life coach.

Self-belief was a missing ingredient in my life for as long as I can remember and I spent a lot of time hoping something would magically alter its course. I lived as a victim who needed rescuing instead of realizing that I had a powerful role to play in how my life turned out. I didn't know how to believe in myself, follow my passions or take the steps to create a life that I loved. I didn't believe that I had any real power. Now that I know I do, I am finding a way of living that is easier and I'm starting to reap the benefits tenfold. We always have a choice, conscious or unconscious. We can actively participate in creating our life or just sit back and hope for the best. This is a stage of growth that each of us has to arrive at on our own. It usually happens when we are up against a wall and nothing else is working for us. Although we can teach and encourage each other, change ultimately has to be a choice we make. Cancer was not the only crisis that had come into my life, but it was the one that got me to sit up and really take notice.

After treatment I knew I couldn't go back to my old life. I really did want to live differently, yet I found it difficult to visualize what future me would look like. I struggled with my thoughts which were often self-defeating and I recognized it as an old pattern. I was determined to change and knew that my thinking had to change. As an example, when I first started writing it was just a way for me to express how I felt. It was only when I started to see the possibilities that I got to work. I knew I was on the right track as it flowed quite easily for me and I got lost in the process. All the same I was plagued by old, limiting thought patterns. I didn't believe that I could write a book and I said as much to people I met. This was all new territory for me. I eventually realized that my words would come true if I wasn't careful. Slowly but surely I gained the confidence to own the fact that I was indeed writing a book. Once I wrote a first draft I put it to one side. I needed distance from it as I was still processing the life-changer that is cancer. I was encouraged to write fiction, so I decided to trust the advice and give it a go. I didn't have a plan, but like this book, once I sat down the words just flowed. The book, *The Tapestry of Life,* is a tribute to the power of community. Only afterwards I realized that I had written what I needed to learn. As I found writing, I found a whole new community, a tribe of like-minded people. If I hadn't trusted life and sustained the belief that it was possible, I wouldn't have written anything. I'm sure that is the case for anyone who has achieved something important to them. They understand the power of belief. In Wayne Dyer's words, *You'll see it when you believe it.* By the same token, if we believe that nothing is going to change, that is the result we are likely to get. It can feel scary or exciting. Knowing that fear is counterproductive, indeed destructive, I try now to focus on the possibilities for my life. New possibilities did start to open up, possibilities that I would never have entertained because of my limited view of life. Having read the words of Marianne Williamson, they echoed strongly with me, *Who am I to be brilliant, gorgeous, talented, fabulous? Actually, who are you not to be? You are a child of God. Your playing small does not serve the world.* I no longer wanted to play small. We all have great gifts to share and we're not doing anyone any favors when we don't celebrate them. I think, in Ireland particularly, cultural conditioning has kept many of us from fully inhabiting who we are. However, the fear of being seen as arrogant or full of ourselves only deprives the world of our unique talents. What does it cost us when we feel limited by what others believe we are capable of? What is the impact on our health when we suppress who we really are? Everyone benefits when we live without limits. I love being in the company of people who are totally comfortable in their own skin. The energy that comes from them is infectious.

When I say living without limits, I mean living with a passion to express who you truly are. I mean having excitement for life and a willingness to dream big. I mean letting go of fear and old limiting beliefs and programming; *Living Bravely*, to quote American researcher and storyteller, Brené Brown. At this point in my life, I know it is the only option for me. I have no interest in just clocking in time. I don't mean to be overly dramatic, but I don't see any alternative other than to curl up and die. What did I come here for, other than to be myself in the fullest sense? To me that means following the highest calling of my soul, and although often challenging, I know when I'm doing that and when I'm not. It's like the curtains have been pulled back and there is no closing them. What I could withstand when I was in the dark and struggling just isn't possible anymore. I truly feel a momentum has taken hold of my life and there is no going back.

As I start out on a new path, I have a better grasp of the Law of Attraction. I had read the book, *The Secret*, when I was younger, but I hadn't fully grasped the concept. Life experience, spiritual practice and learning from great teachers have all brought me to a new place of understanding. Seeing results show up has also made it easier to keep going. Now I judge myself less when I slip up along the way because I know I am making progress. I love the teachings of Wayne Dyer and am drawn to the work of Dr. Joe Dispenza. I have watched many of his lectures online. He has written a number of books on this topic including, *Breaking the Habit of Being Yourself, You are the Placebo, Evolve Your Brain* and *Becoming Supernatural*. So too has Dr. Bruce Lipton, author of the bestseller, *The Biology of Belief*. As I researched this topic I found that new science points to this truth. We possess great power within that most of us aren't aware of. We have become so addicted to our minds that we have lost touch with our essence, the deepest aspect of ourselves that is beyond the rational mind, and description. This science points towards possibility and the power to co-create. It gives us a new understanding of the world we live in. I came to much of this realization through my life experience and when I did some research it confirmed what I knew deep down. We are all different and some will look only to science to learn and trust ideas. I prefer to live in a more intuitive way. My growth has come from personal experience and how I have responded to it. It has been challenging, but it has also been very freeing. It has never been enough for me to know things intellectually. I need to experience them. For me, the real learning takes place when I embody it, feeling it in every cell of my body. When I explored the work of Dr. Joe Dispenza, Dr. Bruce Lipton and other scientists, I felt like I had finally found the truth. In *Breaking the Habit of Being Yourself,* Dr. Joe Dispenza explains how our personality is made up of how we think, act and feel, and how our personality creates our personal reality. If we change the way we think, feel and behave, we can change our personal reality. The scientific models of quantum physics, neuroscience and epigenetics reveal the truth of how the universe and life works. I really believe we are on the verge of a whole new way of living and how we understand our existence – a paradigm shift, if we are ready to grasp it. I won't attempt to explain the science, as I am not a scientist, but I will share what I have learnt from my research and what I have personally experienced.

Neuroscience shows us that we can change our brains just by thinking differently. Nerve cells that fire together, wire together. Basically, when we think differently, neurologically we map new connections in our brains. We are not hardwired to always think the same, as was previously thought, and neuroplasticity tells us that when we repeatedly align our belief, feelings, visions and actions, we can experience lasting changes in our brain. We create a new mind. Interestingly, neuroscience was one of the modules on the life coaching course. As clients come to coaching for change, mindset and beliefs are an important aspect of making this change. We did exercises on our beliefs and how to shift them from limiting to empowering. We learnt about resistance, the gremlins that can show up at times of change, the internal dialogue and old habits that can hold us back. We learnt strategies for developing a growth mindset and supporting ourselves as we navigate the change. When we do this for ourselves, we can then help clients put this into practice in their own lives.

The science of epigenetics gives us new evidence that our lives are not predetermined by our genetic makeup. It shows us that signals from the environment affect our gene activity. We are not victims of our genes. We are masters of our DNA. The environment refers to external and internal signals (thoughts, emotions). Our nervous system reads environmental signals. How our nervous system reads the signals depends on how our mind interprets them. So our reality is created by how we perceive things. Our brain releases chemicals that match our interpretation of the signal. These chemicals are sent to the blood, or via our nervous system to our cells, which affects gene activity. I have no doubt whatsoever that our cells feel our thoughts and process them chemically. In his book, *The Biology of Belief,* Bruce Lipton, PhD points out that only about 10% of what happens in our bodies is related to our genes or family history, including our genetic expression. Our health is primarily determined by our environment, and the most important part of our environment is our beliefs. If we believe we deserve to be happy and healthy, we are taking the first step toward achieving that. We have all witnessed how people respond differently depending on their perception of a situation. It could be standing in a queue, on a flight or in traffic. One might be calm, the other stressed. Two people in an identical situation are having a totally different experience of it and consequently a different chemical reaction in their body. One of them has high levels of the stress hormone, cortisol, in their system and the other doesn't. We may all inhabit one planet, but we are each living in our own world, a world that is based on our thoughts and programming. It may be a very simplistic example, yet you get the idea. I have noticed the difference when I choose to go about my day consciously rather than on autopilot.

I'm not suggesting that one experience of stress is going to have serious consequences on our health. I really don't know. However, if our perception of life causes us to live with a pessimistic outlook or stressful disposition on a sustained basis, I believe we are headed for trouble. I know I was. In Dr. Joe Dispenza's words, *Science tells us that such chronic, long-term stress pushes the genetic buttons that create disease. When we turn on the stress response, which we can do by thought alone, and we can't turn it off, we're headed for disease.* So for health reasons alone, isn't it worth cultivating a positive attitude to life? I'm learning that it is possible to change my perception of situations. It is a choice. Along with my thoughts, I must also cultivate positive feelings that match my thoughts. Body (emotions) and mind (thoughts) must align. Ultimately we can then change our lives.

In recent years, following extensive research, the Centers for Disease Control in the United States published its estimate that approximately 85% of illnesses are emotionally based. It's a pretty staggering statistic, yet it totally makes sense to me. Very interested in this research, I read up further. It points out that suppressing or avoiding our instinctive emotional responses to life's challenges will adversely affect our health in the long run. Many scientists and medical doctors have studied and subsequently verified research supporting this. US scientist Candace B. Pert, PhD, in particular, has shown that when we suppress emotions, this can lead to specific cell receptors in our bodies becoming blocked. These blocks then compromise the normal healthy communications between cells, impairing many bodily functions, weakening our normal immune responses and potentially creating illness. Reading her bio, I learnt that Dr. Candace Pert,[1] who died in 2013, was an

> *internationally recognized neuroscientist and pharmacologist who published over 250 research articles and was a significant contributor to the emergence of Mind-Body Medicine as an area of legitimate scientific research in the 1980's.*

She also coined the phrase – *The body is the subconscious mind.*

In 2002, Dr. Pert gave her view on the future of healthcare and I include an extract here:

> *We have coined the phrase "New Paradigm Medicine" to reflect the fact that it uses the established scientific method and will require quantum physics to understand the scientific underpinnings. The terms alternative, integrative and complementary are political, not scientific terms. We believe that New Paradigm Medicine will be fully scientifically validated one day. ... We are not a collection of*

separate organs or systems, but an information network in which our cells are constantly moving from one location to another as they are being formed or replaced, regulated by the molecules of emotion. ...

Thus cancer, in particular, will be appreciated as a disease of the mind as well as the body and treated at centers... where body, mind and spirit are considered. One day, cancer will be cured by interventions that release emotions in a controlled fashion such as guided imagery, art therapy, animal therapy, massage and bodywork, neurolinguistic programing, energy psychology, chiropractic and last but not least music therapy. These will be used in combination – "cocktails" – scientifically optimized and validated protocols by skilled practitioners, and will actually cure or prolong high quality life in many cancers. Whatever the pain, it's actually the brain where it is perceived. Sophisticated biofeedback methods instead of drugs or surgery will be used to treat it more successfully, along with the methods above – and more.

When I read her words, I knew they were true with every fiber of my being. I have an intimate understanding of the mind-body connection after my own experience with cancer and no one can tell me otherwise. I really hope we see a more progressive face to medicine in the future, one that is directed towards the root cause of illness, one that empowers and no longer limits our understanding of our self-healing abilities.

The quantum model of physics states that there is an energetic field where all potentials exist simultaneously. So, as Albert Einstein said, if we want a particular reality, we have to match the frequency of that reality because everything is energy. Our thoughts and emotions are an energy that we transmit to the world and it comes back to us. So the saying that life is like a mirror is so true. When you start to look at your life like that, a lot of things start to make sense. I know that when I found my life a struggle, there was a struggle going on inside of me. I was holding on to unexpressed emotions like grief and anger and they were showing up in my outer world too. Now that I feel more peaceful and connected, there is more flow to my life. So, the overall message for me is that if I think, act and feel as if my prayers are answered and I do this consistently, steady, gradual change happens. Dr. Joe Dispenza explains this:

> *The elevated emotion is the carrier of the thought, as all frequency carries information. It is all about energy. We then are a vibrational match with what we seek and it finds us! This is the moment when we merge with universal consciousness. We have to live, think, feel as if our dreams have come true and only then they do.*

We hold immense power within. It is a natural creative power which is present in everything. I had no idea that I had access to it. Marianne Williamson in her book *A Return to Love* captures this so well – *Our greatest fear is not that we are inadequate, but that we are powerful beyond measure.* I hope a day comes when we let go of small thinking and step into our authentic power.

I will finish this chapter by relating the science to my personal experience. I have talked about the anxiety and stress I felt long before I got sick. I had suppressed my emotions for many years. I struggled to find my voice. This was not always evident on the surface as I like many people was good at pretending and getting on with life. I wore many masks. I have no doubt whatsoever that the stress hormones of cortisol and adrenaline were at high levels in my body for a sustained period of time and ultimately led me to develop breast cancer. All the signs were there. I know it was my body's way of communicating how out of balance I had become. I was feeling unhappy and without purpose. In this agitated state, I was making decisions and in environments that were unhealthy for me and only drained my energy further. I had no boundaries in my life. I was giving a lot more energy than I was receiving and it was costing me dearly. My body became out of balance as I was living a life totally out of balance. I'm very grateful for being given the opportunity to stop, regroup, understand what was happening and set out on a new path. Although I have great respect and gratitude for the medical community who treated me, conventional medicine is all about treating symptoms, while little emphasis is put on the underlying causes and the fact that the body, mind, spirit connection is real. Maybe it is not the role of the medical community. Maybe it is up to each and every one of us to tap into that inner knowing and act on it. I feel greatly encouraged when I read the work of pioneering doctors and scientists like Dr. Candace Pert, Dr. Joe Dispenza, Dr. Deepak Chopra, Dr. Gabor Maté and many others. My direct experience has shown me that everything is connected. As a result I now see new possibilities for my life.

Gift

As I was on the road back to health and started training as a life coach, I began to feel like a whole new world was opening up in front of me. Lessons about the power of thought and emotional well-being kept showing up. I wanted to live a more empowered, creative life and all of the science that I researched was also pointing me to this truth.

[1]Dr. Candace Pert rocketed to fame in the scientific world in the early 70s when, as a fledgling neuropharmacologist, she took on the daunting task of finding the opiate receptor for her doctoral dissertation at the Johns Hopkins School of Medicine. For the next decade and a half she headed a laboratory at the National Institutes of Health which published over 200 scientific articles explaining the discovery of numerous "neuropeptides." The ground-breaking work that Pert did with the opiate receptor was later nominated for a Lasker Award, also known as the "American Nobel Prize," awarded annually for outstanding

medical research.

Pert's discovery of the opiate receptor started a revolution that would later create profound shifts within nearly every field of modern medicine. It would ultimately unite immunology, endocrinology, neurophysiology, psychology and biology into a cohesive theory about how our thoughts and emotions are capable of creating wellness or disease in our bodies. It would explain and validate what Eastern healing traditions, shamans, energy healers and most alternative practitioners have understood for eons.

Eastern philosophy would state that consciousness precedes reality. Western thought espouses the opposite view and has taught for hundreds of years that consciousness, thoughts and emotions are products of the physical brain and have little to do with the body or our health. How many times has the statement, "It's all in your head," been given when no logical answer makes sense, thus suggesting that whatever complaint is being reported by the patient is not real. Pert would say it's all in your "bodymind" and it's all important. She maintains that theories of psychosomatic illness must shift, as we uncover ever more scientific research validating that consciousness is a body-mind phenomenon – www.healingcancer.info.

Chapter 15

Express Yourself

Creativity is the way I share my soul with the world.
Brené Brown

For me Brené Brown's words say it all. We came into the world to express ourselves and live a full life. Creativity is at the heart of who we are. This has been one of the most enjoyable and healing times in my life. I didn't plan to explore my creativity. In fact, I didn't think I was a creative person. I grew up believing that there are creative people and there are people who are not. Then as time passed I found myself drawn to writing and I started playing the piano again. I also returned to knitting which I had loved when I was younger, playing around with patterns and experimenting with color. The child inside was itching to get out and play. It happened instinctively. Whereas I once saw creativity as the preserve of an elite few, now I know that we are all creative beings at our core. We are the products of creative energy and each of us has a unique way of expressing it in our lives. It can be the conventional artistic endeavors like singing, dancing, painting or writing. Really it is anything you do that expresses who you are. That can be gardening, making things, your job, conversation, helping others, how you dress and on and on. It is whatever allows you to express your individuality and have fun with it.

When I started *The Creative Life* course a few months after treatment finished, it opened the door to that untapped part of myself. Margie, who runs the course, has a unique ability to see the true potential in each person and she supportively challenges each one to live up to it. Using Julia Cameron's book, *The Artist's Way,* the course is in essence a spiritual path, initiated and practiced through creativity. One of the basic principles is that there is an underlying, in-dwelling creative force infusing all of life, including ourselves. Aside from reading the book and undertaking the exercises in each chapter, there are two key tools that are the essence of the program, the Morning Pages and the Artist's Date. The Morning Pages are three pages of longhand writing that you commit to every day. It can seem challenging at times and often you may feel you have nothing to say. It doesn't matter. It is basically a stream-of-consciousness writing that no one else will ever see. It is not about becoming a writer. It is about transferring all that is going on inside onto the page, good and bad. It doesn't matter whether it is your frustrations with life, your dreams or that you feel stuck. Putting it all down on paper without censoring helps get beyond the blocks we unconsciously put in our own way. We are getting in touch with our creative self; our essence. It is the divine spark in each of us that is dying to get out and play. It is who we are at our core. The Artist's Date is a block of time, usually one or two hours a week that you set aside to honor your inner artist. That might involve going for a walk, visiting a bookshop, watching the sun set, basically a play date that you go on alone. So let your imagination run free. See it as an opportunity to open up to insight, inspiration and guidance. Our inner artist is a child and you are taking it out to play. In the book, Julia Cameron likens these tools to a radio transmitter – an out and in process. The Morning Pages notify the universe of your dreams, frustrations and hopes. The Artist's Date allows you to start hearing solutions. It has been one of the most worthwhile courses I have ever done. As we still continue to meet every month, the momentum has been sustained. It nurtures me like nothing else.

I also realized that my life up until then had been all work and no play. I suppose as we grow up we are encouraged to be serious and focus on work. I put little value on the importance of downtime and creativity. I found it hard to justify, but it's essential for a healthy, rich life. Finding a way to express what makes us unique is why we are here. Anita Moorjani captures this perfectly in her book *Dying to Be Me – We are here to discover and honor our own individual path.* I never realized the impact when we don't express ourselves. Our light dims, we feel purposeless and lost. We should never be afraid to do what makes our heart sing or to explore and find it. I got glimpses of this throughout my life, but most of the time I felt quite trapped and powerless. I thought the dreams I had were irresponsible and I didn't follow them because of fear. As an example, I always felt quite restricted in a nine-to-five job. Sometimes I had the energy and drive to work late into the evening. At other times I wanted to rest or start work later. I thrive on a level of autonomy and flexibility. I felt like a child having to stick rigidly to set working hours and it didn't suit my temperament. Granted there was a certain amount of flexibility in my particular role, but I knew I had the passion to work for myself. I had the motivation and self-discipline to make it work. At the same time I was afraid and didn't know where to start, so I buried that dream – that is until cancer shook things up. Living a fearful life is far more damaging than I ever realized.

In the words of Wayne Dyer: *When you stay on purpose and refuse to be discouraged by fear, you align with the infinite self, in which all possibilities exist.* This is what being truly alive means. I no longer want to conform to society's or anyone's idea of how I should live. It is important that we all trust ourselves and each other. I now trust my inner wisdom implicitly. It is a compass that guides me and has really anchored me in my own life. While working in the university, I gave presentations in hundreds of schools every year. I did this over a ten-year period and I met thousands of students. I also met parents at events to promote the university. I was always struck by the incredible pressure on teenagers to perform well in their Leaving

Certificate (university entrance) exams and go on to university. Some didn't know why they were doing it or if it was what they truly wanted. Although there are other options, it seemed to be the expected route for a high percentage of students and I saw first-hand the stress it caused for many of them. Ironically, now that there are more choices in life, the path seems to have narrowed and university is seen as the preferred path for most. Surely not everyone is destined for university, nor do they want it. I firmly believe we should fill young people with confidence and self-belief, encouraging them to make decisions that are right for them. When we trust and let them explore, they come to know that they possess everything they need within to make the right choices for their life. It may not be our choice for them and it should never be our choice. On raising children, the Dalai Lama says, *Give the ones you love wings to fly, roots to come back, and reasons to stay.* I see this as helping our children become self-reliant so that they can live their own lives, while at the same time giving them the security of unconditional love and support. Poet and philosopher, Kahlil Gibran, said, *Your children are not your children... They come through you but not from you... though they are with you, yet they belong not to you.* None of us are possessions. It is our birthright to just be ourselves. We all need family and love, but not at the cost of our right to live the life we choose. Each of us has a unique destiny to fulfill and we suffer greatly if we don't honor that. Many successful people never went to university or even finished school. Instead, they followed their passion and creative calling. Although I am a great believer in education, I also believe there are many forms of education. It isn't just a piece of paper from a university which gives us that. The University of Life and our interest in learning supports us too. We learn by following our interests and it will change as we grow and evolve. We learn by trusting ourselves and by following our hearts. For many years I loved my job. Then at a certain point it started to feel limiting. I had learnt all I could and had given as much as I could to it. I needed to make change. Cancer gave me the push I needed to finally take that step and see where it would lead.

We must each find our own place in the world. No one can do that for us. I learnt this from interacting with many young people in my work. I had to remind myself to hold back from giving advice or pushing my opinion. I often heard the words – *You won't make a living doing that. You need to get a proper job.* Those words may come from a place of love and concern, but they are rooted in fear and limitation, not helpful when we are starting out. How do any of us really know that? Truly successful people talk about their failures. They welcome them, knowing how necessary they are and how much they teach us. I firmly believe that if we confidently follow what brings us joy our future is bright. We all came here with a mission and when we are on that path the universe conspires to support us. Expressing ourselves and being on purpose is the key. It is quite simple. If we don't always succeed, that's okay. We have learnt something new, we hone our capacity to bounce back and we can move on. Isn't this the greatest hope we can have for our young people? I loved seeing the positive impact it had on students when they were given space and support to figure out their own answers. Nothing could stop them. This is also what attracted me to training as a life coach. Another fundamental cornerstone in the coaching relationship is – The *client is naturally creative, resourceful and whole.* It is not about advising, directing or telling a client what they should do. They are held as innately capable, and inventive, with the ability to generate their own solutions. They are the experts in their own lives. The coach is there to support them and expect it of them. I have witnessed this personally with clients. It has a profound impact when you believe in a person and encourage them to trust themselves. There is no denying that there is an indefinable, intelligent life force at the center of all living things. Just observing nature will give you a sense of its power. It is the one loving source of all life and we can all tune in and access it.

There is substantial evidence too that expectations shape experience. In the 1960s a professor from Harvard University conducted an experiment, where teachers in a school were told that some of the students were *late bloomers* and that they were about to have a dramatic improvement in their academic abilities. However, the children were randomly selected and were no more special or different than their classmates. By the end of the year, they had not only performed better in the eyes of their teachers, they also scored significantly higher on standardized IQ tests. The teachers' expectations had a significant impact on the students' performance. This same phenomenon is sometimes called the Pygmalion effect in business because of the 1988 *Harvard Business Review* article, "Pygmalion in Management" by J. Sterling Livingston. This essay looks at the evidence for the ways in which expectations shape performance, and Sterling says – *The way managers treat their subordinates is subtly influenced by what they expect of them.* It is a really powerful way to engage with people, expecting the best of them.

Getting in touch with my creativity was also a gift of practicing meditation. It feels like plugging into my power source. Afterwards, I feel calmer, recharged, and I often have new insights and ideas. I now have a practice where I meditate before I write and it has really helped me get in flow. There are also plenty of times when I feel stuck. Then I know it is time to stop and put my attention elsewhere. Life now feels spontaneous, fresher and more exciting. Another side effect of exploring my creativity has been the joy I get from being around children. This wasn't always the case. Although I love my nieces and nephews, I was often so frustrated with my own life when I was younger that I found it hard to relate to them. I believed that life had to be a struggle. I thought I had to push myself hard to be worthy of happiness. It isn't true. Getting cancer forced me to see life differently. As a result I have chosen a simpler way of life. I still have challenges like everyone else, yet I trust myself to live in a way that honors who I am. Now I really enjoy being around children. I love their honesty, wonder and playful approach to life. Being authentic is their natural state. They have helped me get in touch with my inner child. It seems ironic that we spend a lot of time teaching and directing children to fit into the conventions of a world that is far from perfect. Then as adults we spend time healing and trying to get back to that place of simplicity, joy and freedom. Children are free in how they express themselves. They don't have limits on what is possible, dreaming big and having no fear. It has often struck me that we are not here to teach our children, they are here to teach us. Each new generation has something new to teach the world. At the end of this chapter, I put a question to you – *What aspect of your life allows you to express your creativity, feel engaged, in the zone, lost in time?* If the answer isn't clear, I would encourage you to find it. Each voice in the world is unique and longs to be heard. It will bring you great joy, balance out other stressful aspects of your life and feed your soul. If you know, as I now do, that our mind, body and spirit are all connected, then you will know that expressing yourself is not a luxury. It is a necessity for living a fulfilling life.

Gift

When I explored and took time to connect with my creative energy, it changed everything. I started to feel really engaged with life. I had never valued creativity and I suffered greatly because of it. I have learnt that I'm not living life. Life is expressing itself through me. In the words of Eckhart Tolle, *Life is the dancer and you are the dance.*

Chapter 16

The Source Of My Happiness

Maybe you are searching among the branches, for what only appears in the roots.
Rumi

As I started to write this chapter, many conflicting emotions arose. Who are you to write about happiness? What do you know? What research have you done? There are people a lot more qualified than you. Self-doubt reared its head, but I didn't give in. Like every chapter in this book, I don't believe I chose the topics. Although it might sound like an odd thing to say, I honestly had no plans to write anything until the question – *Have you ever thought of writing?* was put to me by my friend Margie. It ignited something in me that I didn't understand at the time. I didn't plan, research or put a structure together. I just felt an impulse to sit down and write, and that is what I did. It has been like this throughout. I get a strong feeling to explore a particular topic, and with no idea of what I'm going to say, I let the title sit on the page until it comes to me. And it does. It flows and ebbs, flows and ebbs. There is a rhythm to it as there is to life. As you will see, my definition of happiness has changed as I have changed and discovered that there is only one, lasting source of contentment or peace.

We all have an innate hunger to find happiness, yet it can feel so elusive at times. Extensive research has been conducted on the topic and new books exploring the theme hit the shops all the time. In my quest to find a more contented way of life, I did my own reading. A common thread I found was the role that good relationships play. I can't argue with that. Relationships with really good people got me through the most difficult periods of my life and have brought me great joy. Having people who accept me and encourage me has absolutely changed my life for the better. This community has greatly contributed to my happiness and I hope that I contribute to theirs. All the same, they are not the source of my happiness. Actually, as I became happier and more contented in my own skin, I started to attract this type of person into my life. As the saying goes, happiness is an inside job. So what do we do, if we need to do anything, to cultivate this state?

From what I can see, there are as many different perspectives as there are people. Our life circumstances and where we are on *Abraham Maslow's Hierarchy of Needs* must play its part. One person might say that satisfying basic needs, like having a roof over their head or three square meals a day, makes them happy. Another might point to family, a sense of purpose or experiences like going on holiday. Curious about the origins of the word, I looked it up in the Online Etymology Dictionary. It lists the word happiness as dating back to the 1520s and meaning good fortune. In the 1590s, *pleasant and contented mental state* was recorded. Interestingly, the word happy dates back to the late 14th century and at first meant *lucky.* An exception to this was in the Welsh language where it meant *wise.* So is happiness, luck or wisdom, or something else completely? In my case I can say that although I enjoy lots of experiences, my happiness hasn't come from them. I appreciate nice meals, conversations and lots more, but I know they are just that, experiences. In fact, I often used activities like shopping, working and a stream of endless doing, to distract me from feeling unhappy. It didn't work, at least not for long. As soon as I was brought to a standstill after my diagnosis, it became plainly obvious that many of the things I had thought would bring me contentment didn't. I had to accept that if I couldn't sit quietly on my own, feeling some level of peace, I couldn't honestly say that I was happy. If

105

that is also the case collectively, then is the pace of modern life and the high level of material consumption just part of our quest to fill some emptiness deep inside? I'm convinced it is. It is no accident that many businesses have lined their pockets on the back of our insecurities and search for the elixir of happiness. They promise us beauty, love, the perfect life and on and on, and we buy into it. They tap into our feelings of inadequacy. They capitalize on the greatest human fear that we are not enough just as we are. I never felt enough just being me. However, things will never fill the void or bring a stable sense of happiness. They can't, because things are temporary and the feelings we get from them are temporary. I know that from personal experience and I spent a lot of money figuring it out. There is nothing wrong with having nice possessions. They are there to be enjoyed. The problem is when we believe they are the answer. We just end up trapped in an endless cycle of consumption. Thankfully, I no longer have the same urge to buy and acquire things like I used to and it's not because I have developed some great power of self-discipline or control, far from it. It has dissipated because I no longer feel any great emptiness inside or need to escape. In fact, I found myself doing a big clear out while I was confined to home during cancer treatment. As I looked around, I saw the remnants of the earlier chapters of my life and I knew they had to go if I truly wanted to move on, and I did. The first step I took was to tackle my clothes. I felt a tinge of guilt as I inspected three wardrobes that were bulging at the seams. I didn't remember buying many of the items and some I had never worn. That will give you a sense of my overindulgence in retail therapy. As I sifted through the hangers I was surprised to find that I had little interest in what I found. Granted I looked and felt very different. My body had taken a pummeling from chemotherapy and surgery, and no amount of clothes was going to fix my distress about my physical appearance. I packed up about twenty black bags and dispatched them to family and charity shops. It felt so good to let them go. Clearing out the clutter in my house was just the physical manifestation of clearing out emotional clutter. It was a huge weight lifted and I felt I could finally breathe again.

Processing old emotions had a seismic impact on me and definitely contributed to my happiness. I received a lot of help as I turned to counselors, healers, workshops, courses, you name it I did it. It was my life's mission for many years. However, it was my experience with healer Pádraig in 2014 that was a game-changer. I can't describe how radically different I felt after that exorcism of emotions. I had always found it very difficult to face and feel emotions, even as a child. Whether they were good or bad, I found them overwhelming and I would do anything to stuff them down. I also easily picked up on others' emotional state and still do. With time I have found healthy outlets for processing the ups and downs of life and grounding myself. I have learnt from many great teachers that the only way through an emotion is *through* it. There is no bypassing it. Now when I feel uncomfortable or irritable, I know that I'm stuck or blocking something that I don't want to feel. When that happens, I return to the practice outlined by Michael A. Singer in *The Untethered Soul,* or I turn to my breath work practice. I let the energy go. Getting into this type of routine really is like a magic pill, as long as you are willing to totally surrender. Although none of us want to feel uncomfortable emotions, trust me, not only will you feel an amazing sense of physical relief afterwards, it will also change your life. We stop projecting our issues when we deal with our own wounds. When we let go of the past we free ourselves. I also have other practices that I follow to keep me grounded and balanced. I journal, meditate, exercise or get out in nature. So yes, finding balance in the realm of emotions has greatly contributed to my happiness.

I have talked about the importance of being present in Chapter

13. If we can't stay present, I don't believe we can be truly happy. Mindfulness was one of the areas I explored a number of years ago. It is now widely promoted as a way to help us stay present, to reduce stress or pain and gain clarity and peace. I attended mindfulness classes and I also undertook the eight-week MBSR (Mindfulness-Based Stress Reduction) program developed by Jon Kabat-Zinn. He is an American professor of medicine and the creator of the Stress Reduction Clinic and the Center for Mindfulness in Medicine, Health Care, and Society at the University of Massachusetts Medical School. I followed the program while reading his book *Full Catastrophe Living*. It helped me find a sense of peace, and grounded me during a turbulent time in my life. Mindfulness practices, though dating back to the Buddha, are now more often taught in a secular way. I suppose it is up to each person to determine what the practice means for them. One side effect is that we fully experience life, because through mindfulness practices and living consciously on a daily basis, we are present to our experiences.

I also attended a sound healing meditation class using Tibetan bowls. During class, and in workshops, I witnessed people releasing old traumas and emotions that were held in their bodies. It had a profound impact on them. This was a defining moment in my life and led me to eventually train as a sound healing therapist. I learnt about Chi (qi), the vital force or life energy which basically keeps us alive. Chinese medicine, acupuncture and other energy healing therapies all work on balancing and enhancing this energy in our body. It translates as *breath* or *air*. When our Chi is out of balance or depleted, it can lead to illness or disease. It can take time to connect the dots, as disease often won't manifest for many years. I was seeing this first-hand with my own cancer experience. It is nature's way of trying to help us heal some part of our life and get our body back to a state of homeostasis. Homeostasis comes from the Greek word meaning stable or the same. In the body, it is controlled primarily by the nervous system and the endocrine system. At one end of the spectrum we have homeostasis and at the other end extreme inflammation. I know which end of the spectrum I was on. Even though I have only the highest praise for the medical profession and the care I received, I was never going to be satisfied with a conventional medicine approach only. I had no doubt about the body-mind connection as I felt it every day in my own life. I needed to understand my illness in a holistic sense and liberate my innate power to heal. This is what gave me the strength and understanding to deal with my cancer diagnosis. One thing I can say for sure is that once I got over the initial shock of having cancer and I accepted it, I entered the most contented period of my life. It continues to this day and has nothing to do with material things. I suppose getting cancer showed me that whatever plans we make can easily be derailed. I still have goals and dreams today; I just don't feel as attached to the outcome. I don't try and control things like I used to. I've started to focus on what energizes me and what I enjoy doing. I try to appreciate being alive every day and live in a more spontaneous way. I understand that happiness is not about getting and having things the way I want them, or the way my ego wants them. It is not about making comparisons or clocking up what I am owed in life so that I am even with others. This is not how life works. Clinging to this idea led to a lot of unhappiness. I now trust the process of life and know that it will bring me what I need. From my experience, the universe has much greater plans for us than we have for ourselves. I was often afraid to dream big. I thought I would be let down. Instead I let myself down and didn't fulfill my true potential. Now, although I live with a lot of uncertainty, my life has started to flow like never before. I don't feel like I'm struggling anymore. I believe that as long as we are looking for happiness we will spend our lives looking. Ultimately, happiness is influenced by our ability to process life as it happens, gratitude, and the curiosity and courage to choose a path of growth and learning. So happiness is a choice in my book. I now choose to live life in a way that supports me, holding a point of view in any situation that makes me happy.

So is there one source of happiness? My experience is yes there is. It has crept up on me in the last few years. I have mentioned many things which have contributed, but it has primarily come from a process of self-discovery and a settling into the stillness at my core. As I lost my old life through cancer – I was not working, or engaging with people in the way that I used to, not looking like I used to, I was feeling very fatigued – I was forced to slow down. I will always know that period as a very significant time in my life. Rumi's words say it best. Back at my roots, in the stillness, I discovered everything I need to live a happy life. I developed new interests in creative endeavors, community, nature and more. I found a purpose and became excited by life. I have never gone through a period so full of uncertainty, yet it has been my happiest. I feel whole when I am in the still place because I am connected to my source. I feel expansive and free. I'm now living a life that is true to me, so I know I will be okay. Living a life that does not reflect who we really are is one of the worst things we can do. It might be an unhealthy relationship that you stay in too long, a job that is a struggle to face every day, people in your life who disrespect you. You get the picture. We all know the feelings that accompany betraying ourselves – anxiety, illness, depression. I will finish this chapter with words that I now try to live my life by. Go within, live authentically, trust the rhythm of life (it does exist) and appreciate the miracle that is your existence. That is a happy, contented life.

Gift

One of the most difficult experiences of my life was the catalyst for entering the happiest period of my life. I slowed down. I let go of my efforts to fit in a certain type of box. I got to know and embrace the *real* me. I started to expand and feel joy. I found my happiness in the stillness and I turn to it every single day to guide and nourish me.

Chapter 17

Understanding A Crisis

The wound is the place where the light enters you.
Rumi

Not long after qualifying as a life coach, I was asked to share my story at an event called *New Beginnings*. It was organized by a lady called Noreen Kiely, a therapist and coach who is passionate about mental health and helping people make positive change in their lives. I felt a strong urge to contact her after reading an article about the event in the local newspaper, so I did. I was starting to trust my inner compass and live more spontaneously. We clicked instantly when we spoke on the phone. Everything she said resonated with me and I really wanted to be a part of the work that she was doing. As a result of our conversation, I was invited to be on the panel of speakers. The focus of the day was on sharing how we had moved past our individual stories and enriched our lives for the better. It was a learning process for everyone involved as we gathered new skills and strategies to help us make change. As I prepared for the event, I spent some time reflecting on what I had learnt from cancer and other life challenges. My experiences had totally changed my understanding of the nature of life and the title of my presentation reflected this. I quoted the words of Rumi, as they were true for me. As I came to the end of my presentation, I said to the audience that no experience in my life had been wasted. I wouldn't change a thing. I would not have been standing there in front of them if I hadn't gone through cancer. I wouldn't have had that story to tell. I would not have had the confidence to speak in public if I hadn't spent many years making presentations in schools. I definitely wouldn't have been able to talk about overcoming personal challenges if I hadn't done so myself. Nothing beats the credibility and wisdom that comes from personal experience. It was Wayne Dyer's book *I Can See Clearly Now* that awakened me to this perspective on life. In his engaging memoir, he takes the reader on a journey through the formative experiences in his life, fork in the road moments, and he reveals the lessons he learnt with the benefit of hindsight.

> *I wasn't aware of all of the future implications that these early experiences were to offer me. Now, from a position of being able to see much more clearly, I know that every single encounter, every challenge, and every situation are all spectacular threads in the tapestry that represents and defines my life, and I am deeply grateful for all of it.*

It has been a long road for me to embrace this perspective. It can still be difficult, especially when confronted with a painful situation, so I'm not suggesting that in the midst of some difficulty in your life, you will immediately sail through it because you know that it will serve some future purpose. I know that nobody could have said that to me when I was at my lowest point. I would not have been able to hear them. I would have resented them and seen them as lacking compassion. We all need to process and go through a difficult period in whatever way is right for us and I'm definitely not one to judge. I slipped up often and repeated old patterns for quite some time. Still, after much suffering, something started to click inside and I was finally ready to let go. For me, cancer was the time when the light got in and I was finally ready to adopt a different attitude to life. My controlling, fearful one hadn't been working no matter what I tried. Still, there is a time for sadness, anger, denial, letting go and finally healing – all stages we go through, and they are necessary. We can't bypass them. However, when the time is right, we can start to look at life's challenges in a different and more constructive way. When we do this, the path becomes smoother and we bounce back quicker from the setbacks that are part and parcel of being human.

Wherever you are now on your life's journey, I would ask you to cast your mind back to a difficult period. Pick one that you have some distance from. Even if it still hurts and you have not fully healed, I would ask you, for just a moment, to suspend all negative thoughts and associations with it. Open your mind and look for an example of how the experience has served you since. Maybe it gave you new skills to handle a situation that you had struggled with. Even if it's hard, I urge you to find even one good thing that has come about as a result. It will not undermine what you went through. Just focus on it for a short while and don't pay any attention to old stories that resurface. If you find this an almost impossible task, it's a sure sign some healing is needed. It may be time to get some support to work through it. It will only hold you back otherwise. However, if you can, focus on something positive that came from it. It will bring you back to a place of authentic power. It could be a job you didn't get and another came along at a later stage that suited you better. It might be a situation you found distressing, which ultimately caused you to establish better boundaries. Maybe you finally walked away from an unhealthy relationship and bet on yourself. I'll share a few of my experiences, aside from cancer, which has been one of my greatest life lessons so far.

Prior to my diagnosis in 2016, I had been living with high levels of anxiety. There was no one cause. I know that now. Everything that happened in my life had to happen and I am genuinely grateful for every single experience. I would not be who I am today if it weren't for everything I went through. In terms of my work, I went from feeling excited by it every day for many years, to eventually feeling burnt out. It was like the life force had drained out of me. I could not stop worrying, and the anxiety stayed with me well into the weekends, often giving me sleepless nights. I could not find an off button even when I was alone. *Welcome to my world,* many of you might say, and yes that seems to be how many of us are living, or existing more like. More was demanded of everyone after the recession hit in 2008 and it is understandable that cracks finally started to appear. We are not machines and nature is surely trying to tell us that today. I had also got involved in a very toxic relationship that further depleted me. I can see that how I was showing up (or more correctly *not* showing up) in life was really the problem. I needed to create a better work/life balance, develop healthy boundaries and assert myself when I needed to. I also needed to honor my feelings. I had no idea about any of these things. I was a *Yes* person all the way. I had never felt enough at the best of times, so I was only too happy to keep giving, while unable to ask for anything that I needed. That difficult period definitely stood to me and I now have an uncompromising approach to prioritizing my well-being. My car accident was a clear wake-up call urging me to change how I was living. Cancer was the final straw a year later when I had not been able to heed the signs. I would urge you to pay attention to any nagging worries and feelings that crop up repeatedly. Pain is always a messenger. The mind-body connection is real and it is there to support you. It is guiding you to higher ground and a healthier way of living that honors who you are.

I struggled for many years to find any good that came from the breakdown of my marriage. It was such a devastation and the physical as well as emotional pain was relentless. I have one particularly vivid memory, not long after we split up. I was still living in the home that we had shared. I was curled up in a ball on the ground, howling. The pain was unbearable. I had no idea how to deal with it, and I couldn't even start to express the depths of my despair. Everyone's experience of a relationship breaking down is different and in my case it was excruciating.

I believe it was down to the deep connection we shared, exacerbated by a fragile sense of self-worth that was there long before we ever met. I had found it hard to connect deeply with anyone in my life although I had lovely friends and family. I felt like an outsider and struggled to find my place in the world. This was obviously what I needed to experience and it has helped me become who I am today, definitely stronger, more resilient and unapologetic for being me. It took me a long time to emerge from that dark place. I was depressed, abused alcohol, isolated myself, overworked, got into unhealthy relationships and was spiraling out of control. Not many people would have known this unless they were very perceptive. I was practiced at concealing how I really felt and keeping the show on the road. Finally, when nothing was working any longer, I had no option but to let go of my old coping mechanisms. I met many people who helped me as I started a slow journey of healing. As I did, I developed great inner strength, self-reliance and courage. I learnt empathy for others who may be going through a painful time. I also learnt that a healthy relationship is about a balance of giving and receiving. It is about contributing positively to each other's lives. All the same, it is not a replacement for learning to stand on my own two feet. I found out that no one, no matter how close we are, can make us feel whole. It is not their role. This is something we need to find on our own. The lessons that I learnt go on and on, all gifts of time and maturity.

So when you start to look at a crisis differently, your life really does take on a whole new meaning. It may seem like an impossible task if you have never looked at life in this way. You may believe that it is all just a series of random happenings. You may believe your attitude won't really change anything. I would strongly encourage you to take a risk and see what happens. What have you got to lose? If you're being hit by misfortune after misfortune, then surely it is worth trying a different approach. Albert Einstein's definition of insanity is *doing the same thing over and over and expecting different results.* I know that I had a lot of insanity in my life and it took a long time for the penny to drop. There is no doubt that every one of us will experience painful episodes at some point. All the same, it is easy to get caught in a loop, repeating the same patterns and responses, even when they aren't working for us anymore. I have done it many times. There are questions that can help us get unstuck. *What would my life look like if this problem was solved? What do I need to change to make that happen? What beliefs do I need to hold? What new behaviors do I need to adopt?* Powerful questions give us an opportunity to explore a different perspective and find more constructive ways to deal with life. It can be one of the greatest challenges – the prospect of change. Do we really care about ourselves enough to go out on a limb and risk trying something new? Can we go beyond our fears? Do we trust life? I have met people who have and I have met people who haven't. I have learnt not to push. We all change when the time is right for us.

When we are trying to make sense of a crisis, there are other questions we can ask ourselves, questions that can help us grow. *What have I learnt from this situation? What is it trying to show me? What have I learnt about myself?* Whether we want to accept it or not, life is a journey of ups and downs, challenges and times of ease and flow. It is always trying to teach us, to help us evolve and show us the way. Even if we can't see it at the time, we gain so much in the long run if we trust it. We can also ask ourselves – *What can I do differently if I face this situation again? How can I improve or change my life as a result? How do I integrate the learning?* These are useful ways of supporting ourselves as we move through life. To me, the experience of life is intended to be one of growth and evolution. We heal and learn from the past and then we carry only the gifts. I know that from a higher perspective, I chose the life that I am living. I chose a life experience that would allow me to expand and evolve. I have no doubt about that. Maybe I could have learnt what I learnt more easily. That is where free will comes in. No judgment – just we do the best we can at any given time, with the abilities we have and what we know. I see myself as a spiritual being having a temporary physical experience, not a physical being having a spiritual experience. Cancer has reminded me to cherish and be grateful for my life and also that there is nothing to fear. For the first time in my life, I had a dalliance with the prospect of death and I felt no fear. I have a strong sense that I have more to do on earth, but if death showed up tomorrow I would be okay with that too. I believe we are all here on earth to awaken – to remember who we really are – an aspect of higher consciousness that came into the body to experience life and fulfill a purpose. When I go beyond my thoughts and settle into the silent mind, I find the answers. Many of my so-called problems disappear, or at least they don't seem as important. I find a way to move through them more easily and I get back on track. This is an ongoing practice for me as the ups and downs of life throw me off balance all the time. It has also taught me not to take everything so seriously. We are here to have fun and enjoy the experience. Even if you have a very different view of life, and spirituality holds no interest for you, I'm sure you still want to live the best life that you can. We all have our own interpretation of what life is about and why we are here. Either way, coming through a crisis more flexible and resilient will stand to you no matter what.

Paulo Coelho's words sum this up for me:

There are moments when troubles enter our lives and we can do nothing to avoid them. But they are there for a reason. Only when we have overcome them will we understand why they were there.

Gift

Understanding that cancer was not just some random happening, but my body trying to communicate with me and lead me towards a healthier way of living was my saving grace. I wouldn't have dealt with it so well otherwise. It wasn't the first life challenge I had faced and I don't think I would have had the strength to come through it unless I could make sense of it.

Chapter 18

Building Resilience

I am not what happened to me. I am what I choose to become.
Carl Jung

As we learn how to process and respond to a crisis, we are developing our resilience muscle. Now more than ever in the world our ability to bounce back is surely being tested. In this chapter I share some of the insights I have gained from my own life experience, my training and learning from people who possess a powerful ability to turn adversity into opportunity. I am conscious that the goalposts have shifted and many are struggling to pick up the pieces in the wake of COVID-19 and all that has transpired in the world since. I count myself lucky that I had the experience of my own life being turned upside down before I witnessed the planet being upended. Dealing with my personal challenges definitely gave me a reservoir of strength to call on when life as we knew it was brought to a standstill at the beginning of 2020. Finding meaning in adversity is my touchstone. When I do that, I can generally find a way through. Difficult times are *always* teaching me something and when I can shift my mindset to embrace that perspective, the battle is nearly over. Viktor Frankl (an Austrian neurologist and psychiatrist as well as a Holocaust survivor), author of *Man's Search for Meaning*, concluded that the meaning of life is found in every moment of living and that life never ceases to have meaning, even in the midst of suffering and death. *Those who have a why to live, can bear with almost any how,* he asserts from personal experience. The book has been identified as one of the most influential books in the United States, and at the time of his death in 1997 had sold over 10 million copies. It is one of the books I turned to when difficult times knocked on my door.

Before we can bounce back, however, we need to acknowledge and feel the pain of whatever has happened. Grinning and bearing it is not the answer. Accepting and feeling our emotions is the healthiest response to any devastation. That is how I try to face up to life now. Even though I felt a sense of relief when I was diagnosed with cancer, it still was devastating. Acknowledging how I felt helped me bounce back quicker and carry only the gifts of the experience. I never thought about being resilient in any conscious way, yet looking back, I can see that I was. I wanted to live differently and I searched out tools and perspectives that would support me. I was also lucky to be surrounded by so many cancer patients who were full of spirit and resilience. They had an uplifting attitude to life that was contagious. They courageously accepted their reality and embraced the present moment. I wanted to face life with that attitude too. If anything, the experience seemed to have given them a renewed vigor for life. For those who were lucky enough to survive, including me, life took on a sweeter taste that would not have been possible otherwise. Cancer definitely inspired me to live bravely and deeply. Facing my fears was very freeing.

We all possess a natural reservoir of strength, although we may not believe it and would prefer not to have to call on it. Nevertheless, it is an integral part of our life experience that we will. Hard times come to us all at some point. We don't have to leave our house to hear about the challenges people face every day. Just turn on the television, pick up a newspaper or go online. Many are dealing with very difficult ordeals and I have often wondered at their capacity to cope. Some seem to do so more easily than others. I know there are tragedies that are unimaginable and the grief must be unbearable for people to carry. I'm in awe of those who do. Support and time to deeply grieve a loss must take place. However, there are also everyday situations in life that can really throw us off balance if we don't have the coping skills to manage. Lest we forget, long before COVID-19, the number of people dealing with anxiety and depression had rocketed in Ireland. I was accustomed to regularly hearing stories of teenagers being prescribed medication to manage their anxiety. I know there is a place for medication in our health care system. It just doesn't make sense to me that it would become the norm for dealing with typical life problems at such a young age. I was offered antidepressants and sleeping tablets at different points in my life. Not very often, but more than I would have thought necessary. The first time was after my marriage broke up and I was in a dark place. I didn't take them. I knew on some level that what I was going through was a grieving process, and it is a process. This was my personal decision and I know it is not necessarily the right decision for everyone. It suited my temperament and was a personal choice. Someone else may need medication to help them keep their head above water while they process challenging emotions. Either way, bypassing our emotions is not the solution. It invalidates them and we only suffer more as a result. We also miss out on the opportunity to grow and develop new life skills that will help us in the future. I just knew that overriding my body's natural response to being out of balance didn't feel like a healthy choice. There was nothing wrong with me, other than I am a human being experiencing what it is to be human. I needed time to be heard and to heal. Drugs would have just masked what was going on and the emotions would eventually reappear at some point in the future. Ironically, I did take drugs as alcohol became my anesthetic for quite a while. Eventually I found the courage to face the pain. It was truly liberating to discover my innate capacity for healing and no longer need a crutch. This healing capacity is available to all of us. I was also offered sleeping tablets when I was finding work very stressful. I wasn't sleeping and felt exhausted. I chose not to take them, partly because I was afraid of becoming addicted to them. At the same time, I knew that sleeping tablets were never going to be my answer. I could survive sleepless nights and if things got worse I would take action, but I didn't want it to be prescription medication. This is just my experience. In no way am I judging or insensitive to anyone who makes a different choice. There is no right or wrong. We are all doing the best we can. I just trusted what felt right for me at the time and everyone else must do the same.

My instinct is that the epidemic of anxiety that has dogged us for many years is directly linked to our disconnection from ourselves and the planet. I know that was the case for me. I never felt enough and I know that many people don't. I didn't feel seen or accepted for just being me. I didn't think I mattered. The irony is that I never accepted myself or felt I was enough, so I couldn't really expect it from anyone else. As a result, I projected my low self-image into the world and it was just mirrored back to me. Interestingly, now that I have a much stronger sense of my true self, it is no longer really an issue. It hasn't helped either that we live in a world where we are encouraged to look for external validation to cultivate our sense of self. Whether it's our bank balance, our weight or our number of followers on social media, they are held up as a measure of our worth. Yet this is not the case. We are none of these things. We are so much more. Rampant consumerism is surely part of the problem too and very convenient for some that it is seen as the answer. It never is. I had to go deeper to connect with who I really am and take back my power. The pace of life and lack of downtime has contributed too I believe. We all witnessed day-to-day life come to a standstill when we were in lockdown. If I was to take one message from the virus, and I believe there are many, it was to slow down and go within. It is only when we stop that we can process life and heal. It is in the stillness that we make contact with the heart of who we are. It is where we find our inspiration and grow. It is how we give our system time to recalibrate and recharge. Despite the challenges, I don't think anyone can argue that having downtime was a silver lining to a difficult period. Whatever our personal situation, slowing down and having time to be with family, with ourselves – *being* rather than *doing* – all tipped the scales in a healthier direction. It reminded me of being a child. We weren't tied to rigid schedules apart from school. We hung out and played. There was plenty of idle time and little anxiety, a stark contrast to our modern world where everyone is scheduled to within an inch of their lives. It appears that the progress we hoped for and a better quality of life hasn't necessarily materialized. Many feel trapped in lives of endless work and commitments, having very little free time and for a lot of people less money. We have become human doings rather than human beings. I do hope that the lessons of COVID-19 will not be lost on us. I don't believe they will.

Now that our reserves of resilience are being called upon even more, how do we nurture this quality so that we can navigate what life throws at us? I'll mention what helps me and what I have learnt from others who handle adversity well.

Attitude

I naturally had a positive attitude towards cancer from the start. Instinctively I just knew that it was going to dramatically change my life, and for the better. I definitely couldn't keep living as I was living. For a long time I had ached for anything that would interrupt the trajectory it was taking and catapult me in a new direction. Now here it was. You might imagine that I should have been able to make change without a life-threatening diagnosis. I wasn't. I was burnt out and beyond that. I feel nothing but gratitude to cancer as it was the catalyst I needed to shift gears. My attitude totally changed my experience and I know this can be the case for anything in my life. I was learning how to reframe my experience. Albert Einstein said: *We cannot solve our problems with the same thinking that created them.*

Becoming conscious of the power of my attitude has definitely shaken things up for the better. I know I always have a choice in every situation. I now genuinely see life as happening *for* me, not *to* me and that is a momentous shift. Just think of it. Every single thing that is happening in our lives is happening to help us grow, evolve, and reach greater heights. Although it can be very challenging at times, life is not out to get us. Nothing could be further from the truth. I'm not saying that life doesn't involve pain. We all know it does. Pain is a side effect of growth, but it does pass. It is how we expand and live greater lives. When we deny and try to avoid this aspect of life we get stuck and suffer. I have to keep a check on my attitude all the time. If I find myself catastrophizing, blaming, judging or criticizing, I know I have some work to do. Our attitude is just a by-product of the thoughts that we think over and over again. If your attitude is not improving your life, then it's worth cultivating one that does. Remember that you are not your thoughts. The very fact that you can observe them means that you can't be them. The practice of meditation is a very effective way to be reminded of this. We all have the ability to consciously choose our attitude in every moment. When we choose one that supports and nurtures us we move through life more easily.

Processing life as it happens

When we face up to life as it unfolds and digest our experiences in the moment, we are making a healthy choice. Then we come to life fresh and equipped to deal with what shows up. When we stuff down what feels uncomfortable, it is guaranteed to come back and bite us at a later date. I can testify to that. There is no bypassing life. Suppressed emotions have nowhere to go when we swallow them and they will eventually manifest when our limit is reached. They can resurface in different ways. It may be physical or mental illness, addictions or compulsions. I'm sure we can all remember occasions when we have overreacted to a situation because our unresolved traumas were triggered. I definitely can. On a day-to-day basis, do your best to process life as it happens. If something comes up, don't push it down with food or alcohol or some other drug. Don't rush to busyness as a distraction. Get it out quickly. You will feel an awful lot better if you do. Find safe ways to do this for you and others. Get support from a professional if you need to. This might go against what you have been conditioned to believe about dealing with life. We are programmed to bury difficult emotions and it only adds to our feelings of inadequacy. It causes huge suffering and can be debilitating long term. It greatly diminishes our capacity to deal with other challenges when they show up because they are just compounding the pain and suffering that is already there. At a certain point, it becomes too much and we reach the tipping point. We can no longer outrun life. We break down or we get sick. We all know what happens. However, if we can cultivate ways of dealing with life as it happens, we greatly improve our capacity to transcend whatever challenges come our way. Then we are truly free to live from a place of authentic power without any fear. We are unstoppable.

A sense of humor

Problems can feel less overwhelming if we can find humor in them. Gallows humor didn't get its name for nothing. Even in the darkest times humor can be a great release. Laughter can definitely release a buildup of nervous energy and recharge us. I never came across as much humor as I did on the oncology ward. I always had mixed feelings about going to the hospital for treatment. One part of me dreaded facing the toxic infusion, yet another part of me looked forward to the belly laughter that always accompanied my appointments. A good laugh is a great medicine for anything and it always outweighed any discomfort I felt. I used to take life way too seriously. Laughter and humor don't stop us from doing what we need to do in life.

We continue to play our part in the world. We just do it in a way that is fun. Being serious doesn't mean that we are any more diligent or effective. In fact it's probably quite the opposite. When we feel calm and relaxed, we make much better decisions. When I'm light and playful, answers come more easily and I make a positive contribution to the world and those around me. We're here for a short time and we can take nothing with us, so better to focus on enjoying the roller-coaster ride that it is.

Get creative

When we are flexible, we move through life more skillfully. Holding on to fixed opinions and ways of doing things only hampers our progress. I always suffer when I fight with life and refuse to go with the flow. If you view life, like I now do, as an adventure with lots of possibility as opposed to uncertainty, it changes the playing field. Knowing this, we can develop lots of skills and techniques to help us handle what shows up. *What's another way that I can look at this? What is this teaching me? What approach can I try to get a different result next time?* These types of questions can lead us to new discoveries about ourselves. We get in touch with our adventurous side. I'm not talking about being falsely positive. I mean being authentic and genuinely in the mode of wanting to learn and find new ways of navigating life. It was only when I let go of fear and was willing to step into the unknown that my creative side emerged. We don't have the capacity to access our creative powers when we are stuck in the rigidity of fear.

Finding meaning

I find meaning when I am willing to learn and take responsibility for my life. I find meaning when I am able to forgive others, when I stop blaming and am willing to let go of the past. I find meaning when I stop identifying as a victim. You may or may not embrace the spiritual dimension of your life, but personally I can say that it has changed everything for me. It wasn't a conscious decision initially, although I have always had an attraction to the mysterious side of life. I see it as an amazing gift that some part of me was willing to go beyond a difficult physical experience and understand it in a deeper way. In truth I had no choice. It just happened naturally. When we find ourselves up against a wall and there is nowhere to turn, we have a life-changing opportunity. I was relieved to let go and accept what was happening. I was also hungry to find a more meaningful way of living. With time, I developed a real connection with a sacred power and it saved me. This is where I now go to find the energy to deal with life's challenges. I know that whatever is happening is happening for a reason. I may not understand it at the time, but I'm willing to trust it.

Holding space

I think this is one of the most important things we can do for each other. When we hold space for another person, we are supporting them to become self-sufficient, competent and capable in their own lives. We act as a container for the overwhelming feelings they may be dealing with. It is an empowering way to be there for each other during difficult times. It is not about action and doing, although that is often needed; it is more important than that. The person can simply be and express whatever comes up, sit in silence or get angry. You are the steady presence in which they can breathe and do this safely. They feel like they matter and are supported. It is not always easy as our desire to fix or help can get in the way. This is not what is called for. We all need an environment where we are safe to feel what we need to feel. We don't have to worry about how we are perceived or that we will be told what to do. I think this is one of the most empowering ways we can support each other and it is a real way to foster resilience. When we are truly seen and acknowledged, great healing takes place. During my own dark days, I experienced this when in the company of the right people who could just be with me. I felt like I mattered. It was uncomfortable initially as I was not accustomed to letting myself be vulnerable in this way. However, the impact it had on me and my ability to move on with my life was incredible. It is not always easy to hold space for someone else. We have to be strong and ready to witness their emotions. If we're not feeling on solid ground ourselves, it can shake us when we meet someone who is struggling. At some point, we will all be called on to hold space for others and we will need them to do the same for us in our time of need.

We are all innately resilient. Even if life's knocks throw us off track for a while, we can bounce back even stronger. I believe it is a quality that is intrinsic to our nature. We just need to nurture it. Think of a baby learning to walk. They take their first step, fall down and bounce back up to try again. They don't give up and think that they are never going to learn to walk. They keep going. Each time they fall, they have made progress across the room. They are never starting in the same place. Eventually they get there. It is the same with life. We never stand still. The choice is whether the experience causes us to get stuck and give up, or move forward and feel empowered. It is we who ultimately choose who we become.

Gift

Learning from life's challenges has absolutely helped me cultivate resilience. I wouldn't be where I am without having gone through them. It definitely helped me when COVID-19 sent us into lockdown. Despite initial moments of adjustment, my overwhelming feeling was one of calm and acceptance. It was a great reminder that we have little control over what happens in life. We can only control our attitude and how we show up in the moment. That is where our real power lies.

Chapter 19

Shine Your Light

It is never too late to be what you might have been.
George Eliot

The words of George Eliot struck a chord when I turned fifty a few years ago. I had no plan to be heading into uncharted territory at this stage of my life, but now I'm glad at the way things have turned out. As a teenager, I had imagined that I would be living a very different life at the turn of the century. I would be thirty-two and just assumed that my future would involve marriage, children and a career I enjoyed. Naïve maybe, as none of us know what lies ahead. Yet picturing a bright, happy future at that age is to be expected. Part of that picture did materialize. In the year 2000, I was still married and working in the bank. In fact I had just got married in April 1999 and I had been promoted at work. Conditioning led me to believe this was my path for life. Most people I knew seemed to be on that track and I didn't know many who aspired to anything different. It was an accepted recipe for a happy life. For many it might be, but my life was not destined to play out like that. When my marriage ended in 2002, I struggled to make sense of everything. I had no idea where I fit anymore. I had always felt like an outsider and now life was confirming it for me. It was only when I eventually met others whose lives didn't fit into neat little boxes that I started to feel a sense of belonging. I had always tried to conform as I was afraid of being judged or rejected for being different. Cancer was reminding me to just be myself. It is because of cancer, not in spite of it, that I am now living authentically. Today I am drawn to people who live fearless, honest lives and are not afraid to shine their light.

Everyone deserves this opportunity. We all came here to be ourselves and I can say for sure that it is never too late.

Cancer was a necessary disruption to my life and as I was recovering I had a lot of time to reflect and let go of the past. As the old me dissolved there was no going back. I had to start from scratch and it felt like a now or never time. Turning fifty probably upped the ante as it started to hit home that time was moving on. If I didn't take the initiative, trust myself and follow my heart, I was going to end up struggling again and feeling very frustrated and bitter. I knew that nothing would change unless I changed. Learning about the law of attraction got me tuned into the power of my thoughts and emotions. I became conscious of the words I used and the things I said. I did my best to let go of complaining and gossiping. I realized that lashing out at others was only a distraction from focusing on me. It was self-destructive and lowered my energy. I started to become aware of my point of attraction. We don't attract what we want, we attract what we are. We align with it. Realizing this really shifted my perspective. We experience the equivalent of whatever we are emitting into the universe. When I'm being judgmental, I feel judged. When I'm being kind, that is what I see in others. In the early days my energy levels were low and I could instantly feel the impact when I was in surroundings that were draining or negative. I was exhausted afterwards. When I consciously chose to be in more uplifting environments, I left feeling recharged and inspired. It was instant and very real. Now I care about myself enough to care about my surroundings. I credit the words of Anita Moorjani for helping shift my perception of the world and myself. *Love yourself as if your life depends on it, because it does,* she said. From a death sentence with cancer, she is now thriving today. You may not have heard of her, unless you have been diagnosed with cancer. She wouldn't be on your radar; understandably so. Her words encourage us to shine our light in the world. When we love ourselves enough, we take time out to reflect, dream and take action. If you answer yes to any of the following questions, you are ready.

- Have you a strong sense that there is more to life?
- Do you feel a hunger to step into the highest version of you?
- Are you tired of standing in the shadows?
- Are you ready to let go of fear and step into the unknown?

Here are some of the steps that I took as I tried to imagine future me. Going through this process definitely helped me realize how important writing is to me. The prospect of becoming a writer and published author was something that I had never, ever considered. Now I feel like I have found a missing piece of the puzzle and I'm sure there are more to find.

Tune in to what makes you tick

You might be very clear on this already. Even so, there is no harm taking time out to reflect. It definitely took me a while to slow down and get in touch with myself in a new way. It is in this atmosphere that we find our purpose. We mine the depths of our being for treasure. It is there in all of us just waiting to be discovered. Answering the following questions helped me tune into my gifts and natural abilities. You might surprise yourself by uncovering something you had forgotten or skipped over as unimportant. Our life history always holds the clues. You might even find a limiting belief that is blocking you from many great possibilities that are just waiting for you.

- First think of times when you were at your happiest in the past – What age were you? What were you doing? Who were you with? What is the memory that has stayed with you? When did you feel energized and enthusiastic? What did you look forward to doing? It doesn't matter if it was work or pleasure. What rocked your boat?

- Now, examine your present. In your day-to-day life, what are you doing when you feel in the zone, lost in time, energized, excited or contented? What do you look forward to doing in your daily life? Is there anything that you look forward to? Has it changed from the past? Really tune in to the times that you feel very much you and free of anxiety.
- Finally, reflect on who you have been for others in your life – family, friends, colleagues, acquaintances. Are you the advisor, the optimist, the calm in the storm, the reliable rock they can lean on, the ideas person, the facilitator, the catalyst? What do people look to you for? This gives you a good idea of your gifts. What do people say about you?

It can be helpful to journal about this. Give the answers time to reveal themselves. It can be days later that I get sparks of inspiration or nuggets of wisdom. It is usually while I'm driving or in idle mode. They can be about anything. Now I carry a little notebook with me. It is full of scribbles and words, many that have helped me make some major decisions, move forward with an idea or even find the next chapter of my book!

Visualize your dreams

When we are not living consciously and on purpose, life can feel like it is just happening to us and we are at its mercy. When we have a vision or a dream to aspire to, it gives us a strong foundation. For many years I was rudderless. I just wanted to escape the life that I was living. Once I set an intention, life started to make sense. Intentions become thoughts, which turn into actions and then results. Be brave. Don't hold anything back, no matter how impossible it seems. Write about it, think about it, or draw a picture. You could make a vision board, by collecting images that appeal to you. It doesn't have to be really detailed. It could start with words, affirmations, colors, shapes, any images that you like. You can build on it over time and flesh it out. There are many online resources available to help you create your personal vision board. Do some research and find what approach works best for you. I'd recommend keeping it simple and true to you. The more you focus on it, the sharper the picture will become in your mind. Revisit it from time to time. Taking another look at your dream, imagine you have achieved it:

- What does it look like?
- Who are you with?
- What are you doing?
- How are you feeling?
- What need/desire is being met?

When you have a clear picture, imagine what achieving it would give you. How would it benefit you and others? Don't overthink it at this stage or let your critical mind get in the way. Don't dismiss anything that comes up. You can return to it later. Go with what comes into your heart. This will give you clues. If your first thoughts are about money or fame, keep going. This is starting at the end and is just your mind talking. It is not necessarily what your heart desires. Take a moment out when you find yourself overthinking. When you start to worry, you come from a place of lack and that will limit you before you even get started.

When I was ready, the first thing I did was an online course with Irish fitness expert and motivational speaker Pat Divilly. It was called *Confidence and Clarity in 30 days*. I had just finished treatment and felt I needed to focus on what I wanted for my life. There were many exercises over the thirty days, but I really liked the exercise called, *Draw your life twelve months from now*. He asked us to think in terms of our health, career, personal life, relationships and self. I was surprised at what I drew. I developed the same picture eight months later as part of my professional training to be a life coach. It hasn't changed much, even today. In fact some of it has already materialized. In one aspect of the picture I was writing and I am now doing that most days. Another aspect was me in nature and I now spend at least an hour every day in the outdoors. This is an exercise I regularly return to and will continue to do so. It has been instrumental in getting me on the path that I'm now on. Focus on who you want to be rather than what you want to do. Cancer was the impetus for me to change my life for the better. A crisis can be a starting point. As a result of my experience, I felt a deep desire to tell my story, to spread a hopeful message, to share another way of relating to life. I wanted to pass on what I had learnt and empower others who may be struggling. I wanted my life to be about service. That is why I trained as a life coach. That is why I learnt different forms of healing. That is why I am a public speaker. That is also why I write. I didn't plan to write a book. I knew who I wanted to be. What I would do came later. It may change again in the future depending on what life brings. When we focus only on what we want to do, we can close ourselves off from far greater possibilities.

Another helpful exercise was doing a Full Personal Review. This was part of the training to be a life coach. The purpose of the exercise was to provide us with honest and direct feedback about how we're experienced in the world. It was about raising self-awareness and identifying the information that we needed to help us become a better coach. We took time to develop the questions as we wanted to get answers that we could use to improve our lives. We asked a minimum of twelve people to complete the survey. They could be family, friends or colleagues. It was important they knew us well and wanted the best for us. It was a bit daunting to start with. I felt like I was fishing for compliments and also afraid of what I might hear. It turned out that there was great synergy between what I dreamed for my life and how others saw me. I also got some great ideas and suggestions; tangible things I could do to bring it all to life. As this exercise may not be possible for you to do, you could ask a few trustworthy people in your life for their input. It is likely that they see talents, natural abilities and skills that you may not be aware of. We all have blind spots. Even if you don't agree with what they say, just let them speak. You don't have to act on anything that doesn't resonate with you. You might learn something new about yourself. You might get some clarity and direction for your life. It may help complete the picture that you have drawn for yourself.

At the risk of repeating myself, try to stay focused on who you want to be, rather than how you will make a living. You need to be free to dream first. Otherwise you will worry. Fear can paralyze you. It nearly stopped me in my tracks altogether. It will become clear in time. Maybe it won't mean changing career straight away, or at all. Maybe it will involve refocusing on an aspect of your job that fulfills you or another aspect of your life that you enjoy. Or it could mean you look for an alternative job. Either way, the process will give you clarity and help you develop new self-awareness. It may help you uncover new insights that will prompt you to change. I know it is not possible for me to do a job that is only about a paycheck. I must find meaning in it. I must be able to express who I am. I must be of service. That is what I have chosen for my life. It is what now guides my decisions.

Bring your dreams to life

Be open to new possibilities. In this step we bring energy to what we have visualized so that we can create it. Let's say you can see what your dream life looks like. What next? Maybe it feels a bit overwhelming and you don't know where to start. Maybe you don't feel you have time to devote to it. Take a breath. Start small. Let's say for example, you discover that working with children is what you really want to do. You connect with them very easily and enjoy the fact that they are still very much in touch with their true nature. They respond really well to you too. You dream of owning your own crèche (day care). Yet you feel daunted by the idea of trying to set up your own business. So how can you bring your dream to life? Maybe you start by doing some voluntary work with groups that work with children. You could talk to people who run a crèche to get an idea of what's involved. You can enquire about training. Maybe you will end up running your own crèche or maybe you will decide to spend more time with the children already in your life; you will offer to babysit or do something completely different, like volunteering with a charity that works with children. Either way, you will find a way to bring your natural gifts to life in a way that energizes you and makes you feel alive. Don't have fixed preconceptions of what your dream must look like. We don't always know the best way to bring it to life, but life will show us if we trust it. Also, by taking small steps in the right direction, you are putting yourself in situations that may open up new opportunities.

What else can you do?

- Stay focused. Keep your thoughts positive and imagine your dream coming to fruition. Keep it like the background music to your life. Look for opportunities and say yes to situations that bring you closer to it. Don't hold off for the perfect job or right timing. Just be open to new experiences that align with your dreams. Trust me. If you are open and alert they will show up.
- Bite-sized chunks. Don't get overwhelmed by focusing on how big a challenge it seems. Just take baby steps. Often the small things that we do regularly over time end up having the biggest impact.

- Keep your energy high. Start becoming aware of the interactions and activities that energize you and those that drain you. Watch your mental diet. What sort of news and media are you consuming? Become more discerning. Say *No* to situations that bring you down and start saying *Yes* to anything that raises your vibration. This is your personal point of attraction. If you are feeling frustrated and angry, you will likely find yourself surrounded by people who are on that wavelength. That's how energy works. When you feel in flow and at ease, the same applies.

- Be aware of the balance of giving and receiving in your life. I know this is where I struggled and I think many people do. We believe that if we give all the time, we will be worthy. We will feel needed and important. However, nobody can give of themselves all the time. If we don't watch the balance we are left with an empty tank and may get sick. We need to be able to receive in life too – to say yes to offers of help and support. I used to find it almost impossible to accept help and it nearly killed me to reach out. The helping professions place a big emphasis on this. I talk more about the importance of self-care in Chapter 21.

- If your life is already busy and chaotic, you may feel you can't afford to take time out just for you. I'd suggest focusing on what you need to stop doing first. You might need to challenge some engrained conditioning. Oftentimes we are caught in a limiting belief system and we do things habitually that are not serving us. Be gentle with yourself. This is not about judgment. It is about finding sustainable and healthy ways of living. Personally, I have found that investing in a consistent meditation practice has benefited me in ways I could never have imagined. Life is not really about what we are doing but who we are being. If you are finding it difficult to say *No* to something in your life, maybe consider why. What are you getting from the situation? If it's not working for you, maybe now is the time to consider making a change. If you are struggling with this, it could be helpful to work with a counselor or coach.

Then let go and trust the process of life to bring you what is right for you. This is co-creation at its best. Maintain focus, keep your energy high, but also be flexible and alert. The universe is always pointing the way. I see it every day in my own life. Although we may not be able to control the future, we can shape it and decide how we will show up to meet it.

Finally, find your tribe. They will nurture you and help you shine your light even brighter. We all need to be seen, understood and to know that we matter. We need people who get us, support us, encourage us and believe in us. We can't do it on our own. My own journey has involved a whole new community of people turning up. I know that I wouldn't be where I am today without them. I wouldn't have had the energy to keep going when doubt crept in. Take a look at the people you spend time with. Do they reflect what you value? Do they add something to your life? Do you feel good after spending time with them? Do you come away with new ideas, a smile and renewed energy to keep going? No one else can take ownership of your life. No one else knows you like you do. No one else can shine like you do. You have something unique to offer the world and it is the greatest thing you can do for yourself and humanity – shining brightly as the highest version of yourself.

Gift

Once I took ownership of my life and made conscious choices, I started to feel a strong sense of purpose. Life experience led me to this point. I now honor who I am and I am not afraid to shine.

This is not about ego, but about responding to the calling to use my gifts and life experience to be of service. This is why I am here. This is why all of us are here.

Chapter 20

Living An Abundant Life

Abundance is not something we acquire. It is something we tune into.
Wayne Dyer

On the rare occasions that I thought about abundance, it was only ever in terms of material wealth. I had no understanding of its true nature or any idea how to live abundantly. I held an unconscious belief that it wasn't my destiny to have what I needed or wanted and I thought it impossible to live without the worry of making ends meet. If things came too easily I almost felt guilty. I wasn't deserving of them. That may sound a bit crazy, but I really felt like that. Writing this chapter has been a bit of a light bulb moment for me. I struggled with it for quite a while. It's been uncomfortable, because I've been forced to dig deep and uncover this really limiting belief. In the end I was close to dumping the chapter altogether as it felt superficial and didn't ring true. Instead, it has turned out to be a really worthwhile exercise to persist. It has taught me so much about myself. It has pushed me to address this faulty program that I was running inside for years. In a way it is a relief to come to this realization. I wasn't consciously going through life thinking this or even aware of it, yet it explains so much to me now. I found it difficult to ask for help or to accept it when offered. At times when I was earning a good income I felt uncomfortable and I was quick to spend it. No doubt that feeling fueled my obsession with retail therapy. It was a vicious circle. I pushed myself harder and the more I did, the less time I spent appreciating all that was good in my life. I was stuck in a world of scarcity where there was never enough. This program was deeply embedded in my psyche. It took me a long time to realize that my relationship with money was unhealthy and a direct consequence of my low self-worth. More importantly, I learnt that abundance is about so much more than financial concerns. The very nature of life itself is abundance, so if I suppress my true nature or hold back from living at my fullest expression, I'm definitely coming from a place of lack.

My rigid view was definitely challenged when I was diagnosed with cancer at the age of forty-seven. Once I settled into the rhythm of treatment and let go, life took on a totally different flavor. My best moments (and they really were some of the most contented of my life up to that point) were doing the simplest but most rewarding things – connecting with like-minded people, sitting in nature, going for a walk or just doing nothing, almost a mortal sin in my eyes before then. Now here I was totally absorbed in experiences without any distraction. My mind didn't have the capacity to entertain worries about the future or regrets of the past. I was only capable of dealing with what was right in front of me. I shifted from skimming along the surface of life at breakneck speed to plunging into the depths of every experience. I was *in* life in a way that I never had been before and to this day it has mostly remained like that. I experience my reality completely differently now. It has changed how I view abundance and it has definitely upped my appreciation of just being alive.

You might argue that life is a rat race and there is no time to stop and smell the roses. That seemed to be the prevailing attitude before the arrival of lockdown in 2020. It was definitely my outlook before I got sick. I thought I was wasting my life unless I was doing and running. I couldn't see a way off the treadmill until eventually I fell off. I didn't realize that I had a choice. I could just step off. I was full of fear and I thought that my life would fall apart. It did fall apart and it had to. That was the gift. It was only then that I discovered the essence of being fully alive. I learnt that abundance is about so much more than material wealth. I reprioritized what was important to me and I cut my coat according to my cloth. It hasn't always been easy and I still have the same life problems that everyone has. What has changed is that I now approach them differently. I'm not saying there is anything wrong with material things and being financially comfortable. They should be enjoyed for sure. They are part of the experience of life. It is when the accumulation of money is motivated by the fear of not having enough that there will never be enough. It is a scarcity mentality and all the money in the world won't fill that hole. There will never be enough of anything – enough time, support, love, and the list goes on. You might laugh and say that you would like to have that problem. You might say that it would diminish your other problems. Maybe it would, maybe it wouldn't. As I said, there were times in my life when financial concerns were not a real issue for me, yet I was at my most miserable. That myth has been busted for me for sure.

While going through treatment I spent a lot of time reading and searching out people who looked to have mastered the art of living well, people who were living rich lives of purpose. As I did, it became crystal clear that it was about their *why* in life. Truly contented people have a *why* that comes from a place of love not fear. It comes from the soul not the ego. I was reminded of a TV program that followed lottery winners. It made for quite depressing watching. Some of the participants had struggled greatly despite their big win. Money had not been the answer to their problems. The financial crash of 2008 was also a good reminder that material wealth in and of itself is impermanent and hollow. I know I'm not necessarily saying anything new here. I just feel called to expose the illusion that so many of us buy into. It controls us. It keeps us small and limited in life. There are plenty of examples of people who naturally ooze abundance. Richard Branson comes to mind when I think of the

word, because of his attitude and sense of energy. In his words
– *A vision of abundance is within reach. It's up to us to create the
world we want to live in, and we all have the power to do so if we set
our minds to it.* Oprah Winfrey is another who I greatly admire
– *When you focus on what you have, your abundance increases. I
started with my breath. Noticing being alive is a good start.* She is
another example of someone who has a real appreciation of
the miracle that is life. They may be exceptional examples, but
you get the idea. I imagine if you asked them their secret, the
concept of abundance would surface. They may not necessarily
use those words, yet they know that every moment is full of
possibility. They tap into the creative power of the present.
They let the future take care of itself. They understand the
power of gratitude. They follow their hearts. They live from
a place of love not fear. They understand being in flow. It is
obvious they don't just pursue wealth purely for its own sake.
They wouldn't be where they are today still doing what they
do if that was the case. They would have no need. You may
look to other people to inspire you. I could name many that I
learn from in my daily life. On every working trip to India I was
struck by the contented demeanor of the people I met. Many
of them had nothing in terms of material possessions, yet they
looked a lot happier than many Western people. I'm not saying
that poverty is okay. It was heartbreaking to see people living in
such impoverished conditions in this day and age. At the same
time, it was a reminder that abundance comes in many forms.
As Wayne Dyer said, abundance is something we tune into.
It's an inner job. It is not something we go out and get. There
are no limits on abundance and someone else's good fortune
does not mean that there is less to go round. There is plenty
of love, money, success, fun, passion, meaning, joy... plenty
of everything. In my frustration, I often drifted into criticizing
or begrudging those who were doing well and seemed to *have
it all*. Yet I knew nothing about their life, their circumstances,

the work they had done on themselves, their commitment to living with gratitude. Isn't that where the expression, *walking in someone else's shoes* comes from? Now I want to learn from people like that.

Today I have a better understanding of how my attitude impacts my life. When I held an attitude of lack, I always felt that something was missing. I didn't have enough. I wasn't enough. I felt empty. I was living from a powerless perspective. Now I see life as full of possibility and I trust that I will be supported as I step into the unknown. Quoting Albert Einstein again – *The most important decision we make is whether we live in a friendly or hostile universe.* That sums it up for me. For a long time the world that I lived in was a hostile world. Now I know it only wants to support me in living at my highest potential.

Life has a natural rhythm and flow. It is innately abundant. The great mystery that is the source of all life is pure creativity and abundance. Time spent in reflection must surely open us up to a sense of awe for the miracle that is life. Nature is a great teacher and my daily walks during lockdown reminded me of this. A tree doesn't hold tight when the autumn winds blow, not trusting that new shoots will appear again in spring. When I tighten up and resist the experiences that life brings me, I straight away feel a sense of lack. When I can find my breath, let go and trust what is unfolding, I relate to life totally differently. In the same way, I see money as the energy of exchange. It is meant to be in circulation through giving and receiving. I'm not suggesting that we don't save or put something aside for a necessary purchase, I speak more of an attitude, a view that life is supportive and generous. A lack mentality paints a dismal picture of the future that causes us to block the flow of abundance. Living consciously in the moment opens us up to opportunity and the generosity of life. We remember that we are all part of one unified system. When this system is not functioning properly the results are devastating. We can see this in the grossly inhumane distribution of wealth around the world, when in reality there is plenty for everyone. It is surely evidence of a system predicated on a lack mentality and greed.

When I look back on my life before breast cancer, I had a good job, I was paid expenses for travel, and I did a *lot* of travel. I had my own house with a mortgage on it, but I had still managed to buy it. I didn't struggle financially. I could pay my bills and yet it wasn't enough. I felt like I was working just to survive and keep my head above water. I didn't feel any sense of fulfillment or joy in my life. It felt like an endless treadmill of activity with no interlude for fun or rest. I was lonely for real connections too. As I have already mentioned, even when I wasn't working, I felt consumed with anxiety and worry, most of the time not knowing what I was worried about. Cut to now and life feels full of possibility. I have no idea what lies ahead. Most of the time I feel so grateful for all that I have received; primarily, connection, creativity, simplicity and flow. I have space and time to really live and appreciate life. That is true abundance. I asked myself recently – *What would I be doing differently if I had more money?* When I really thought about it, I wouldn't be doing anything differently right now. Yes, although I could pay my mortgage off, buy things or go on expensive holidays, it just wouldn't change how I feel deep down. I have qualified as a life coach and want to use these skills to support others. I'm not sure in what capacity or what exactly my work will look like. However, writing this book and telling my story in Cork is all part of the process. I can't see into the future, but I can take the next right step that is in front of me. A greater power knows when it's time for the next chapter and we cannot force things to happen before that time. Everything has unfolded perfectly since I was diagnosed with cancer, despite my worries. If I had given in to my ego mind, I know I would have made fearful, controlling choices. Never in my wildest dreams could I have imagined what has played out so far. There is nowhere to get to.

This is it; the here and now. From now on I just want to do my best to plunge fully into every moment and trust the experiences that show up, as I know they will bring me all I need.

This short poem by author and meditation teacher, Amy Schmidt, nicely articulates the essence of abundance. I believe it is a message that we were getting loud and clear during our time spent in lockdown in 2020. I know I was.

Abundance – in memory of Mary Oliver
It's impossible to be lonely
when you're zesting an orange.
Scrape the soft rind once
and the whole room
fills with fruit.
Look around: you have more than enough.
Always have.
You just didn't notice
until now.

Are you living your life from a place of lack or abundance?

Lack	Abundance
Getting	Giving
Future	Present
Uncertainty	Possibility
Constriction	Expansion
Anxiety	Excitement
Stuck	Flow
Struggle	Rhythm
Push	Pull
Doing	Being
Mind	Heart
Fear	Love
Ego	Higher Self

Gift

Living deeply in each moment and trusting life. Learning to shift my focus from getting to giving. That is abundance. I have found a well of plenty that was always missing from my life. When I live from the ego mind I constrict the flow of life. When I let go and live from a higher place, I see that life is pure abundance and is always supporting me.

Chapter 21

Practicing Self-Care

Self-care is how you take your power back.
Lalah Delia

I now see self-care as an integral part of how I live in my power. I try not to let myself be buffeted by life, but to center myself and tune in to what I need at any given time. We have all heard it said that you cannot give from an empty vessel. I know that I end up feeling resentful, particularly if I'm already feeling stretched and stressed. None of us want demands thrust upon us when we're feeling worn to a thread. Looking after ourselves is essential if we want to be of service in the world. For a long time, I struggled with this idea, believing it selfish and uncaring to put my needs first. It took wise people and counseling to teach me otherwise. When I take time to refuel and recharge, I enjoy being there for others. I spread love and positivity rather than drama and negativity. We all know the difference it makes to our day when someone simply smiles at us or lets us out in traffic. Maybe we smile at the next person we see and make their day, and on it goes. What if we take the initiative? The ripple effect of small gestures is far beyond anything we can fully comprehend. The warmth and care that I received from other patients on the oncology ward made my experience of chemotherapy a very different one to what it might have been. The healthcare system definitely benefits when we take ownership of our well-being rather than always handing over to the medics. For many years, my attitude to self-care had been nonexistent. In fact, I was on a path of self-destruction rather than self-care. I was filled with self-loathing and despair after my marriage broke up. I know it was the catalyst for me to eventually face and heal old wounds.

All the same, it took a lot of inner work before I really got on that path as my motivation for far too long had been discipline rather than nourishment.

Now I see self-care as self-compassion, not pushing, but listening to my body and taking my lead from there. Recovering from cancer and all the associated treatment was a great lesson. My body became highly sensitive. Whether it was food, exercise, people or environments, I could feel alarm bells ringing when something was off. I found this very frustrating. I imagined there was something wrong with me and that I needed to get stronger. I wondered if I ever would. Really I had just become more in sync with my body and it wasn't accepting any more mistreatment. I could pick up on its cues and identify what it needed. I had no choice but to listen. Initially I hit a lot of resistance as I felt guilty for living at a slower pace. I had to let that old thinking go. It was a habit of a lifetime that I had to shed or I knew I'd end up sick again. Cancer was a wake-up call and I didn't need another one. I had a very clear picture of the type of life I wanted to live and I really wanted to look after myself – physically, emotionally, mentally and spiritually.

Nutrition definitely played an important role in my recovery. I'm not a fan of diets or following a very restricted way of eating. I prefer to eat a mainly plant-based diet and natural food. I have a strong sense of what my body wants for fuel and I'm less drawn to sugary, processed foods. I'm not rigid about it, but sugar just doesn't hold the same attraction that it used to. In fact, I often feel sluggish and tired if I overindulge. If my body wants meat, I'll give it meat. If it wants chocolate, I'll give it chocolate. I don't have hard and fast rules anymore. While going through chemotherapy I juiced every morning or at least every morning I could stomach it. About six months after treatment I started to crave vegetables, particularly green vegetables, and it continues to this day. It feels good to be that tuned into my body. I never had been in the past. In the same way that toxic emotions and thoughts weigh us down, I was learning that toxic food has the same effect. Eventually, we don't even realize the impact because we become addicted to and dulled by them.

Our bodies never lie – nothing that we feel is just random. Paying attention and responding accordingly opens us up to a more empowered way of living. We have an inner GPS system that is communicating with us all the time. When you feel stressed or angry, don't you register it in your body? We can ignore it and turn to modern medicine as a cure-all for every ache or pain, but that will never be the case. We will be back to the doctor again and again with the same complaint until we start to listen to how we feel. So how do you really plug in and understand what your body is trying to communicate? Prior to breast cancer, I rarely stopped long enough, physically or mentally, to really listen. I just worried and felt anxious all the time. I went against my instincts and dismissed my inner voice. Now I take time out to meditate, write or go for a walk. It helps me hear intuitive messages. I go beyond the world of logic and mind. Mind has its place, just not as the master of our lives. Our true voice is gentle, often repetitive, but never critical. It is always trying to guide us. In trusting it, we have to surrender and accept that we don't have control over the outside world, only our inner one. This is the relationship I do my best to cultivate. We are co-creators who are at our best when we work with the voice that shows up as hunches and feelings, gently nagging us to take action. It might feel a bit like going into freefall, particularly if you have always tried to control life. When we realize that we cannot force life to do what we want it to do, we are ready for change.

Meditation really is the key for me. When I maintain a regular practice I just know what to do next. It's not easy initially, yet the payoff from connecting with that wisdom only gets better with time. More and more I find myself living from that still place and I feel great peace when I do. When we go deep into the moment we touch the heartbeat of life. That is self-care at its best. We co-create with the wise part of ourselves and do things that support us. As an example, one day I got the strongest feeling that I needed to bring more fun into my life. I had always felt a sense of duty to be working on something, never completely switching off. I had an entrenched belief that if I kept doing more, someone would eventually take me aside and tell me I was enough. I was sleepwalking through life. I hid my feelings of inadequacy under the mask of perfectionism. Lack of self-acceptance was really at the root of my problem. When we trust and value ourselves, we know we are enough and we don't push ourselves beyond our limits. We don't have to prove anything. As trying something musical started to hold new interest, I started a community drumming class. The effect of playing with a group had such an energizing effect on me. As the class progressed and we were introduced to new rhythms, I had to go beyond my mind to stay in time with the group. I got lost in the music and afterwards I walked out of the hall on such a high. It got me out of my mind, into my body and it recharged me.

The desire to be liked and needed can also lead us down a path of self-neglect. Saying *Yes* when you already feel overwhelmed or exhausted, is a typical thing we all do. It is totally fine every now and then, just not healthy when it becomes the norm. Deep down we may not want to say *Yes*, but some wounded part of us is afraid of being rejected if we don't. At work I found it impossible to say *No* to interruptions, more demands, more responsibility, to the point that I was checking e-mails late at night and feeling strung out. I was also good at cramming my diary full of appointments and coffee dates, avoiding stopping at any cost. The connection that I really needed, first and foremost, was with me. I had to find a sense of belonging to myself before I could experience the sense of belonging with anyone else. Now I really enjoy my own company, so much so, that I won't sacrifice it for anything that I know is going to drain me. Never in a million years would I have believed that I would say those words and mean them, but I do. I don't see it as selfish. I have worked hard to get to this place in my life. Feeling contented in my own company is one of life's blessings now. It is where I recharge, refocus and get ready to face the world again.

Something tells me that we weren't designed to live life at the pace we now do. It never made sense to me that my life was meant to be an endless to-do list. Like many of you I'm sure, I overscheduled my life to the point of feeling overextended. I imagine our ancestors didn't operate at the breakneck speed that we now do and didn't speak of stress. Maybe if they did, it was the stress of finding food, shelter and satisfying more basic physical needs. Fight or flight, I imagine, was a lot more literal in its meaning than in today's world. Curious about learning ways to combat stress, especially after facing cancer, I went on my own investigative journey to learn techniques for calming the mind and body. I started a yoga class with a fantastic teacher who brings a truly holistic approach to her work. At the end of the class, she directed us into a restorative pose to recharge and I felt everything switch off, including my mind. The effect was transformative. I felt safe and totally relaxed. As she talked about the parasympathetic nervous system, a light bulb switched on. I realized that for much of my life I had felt on high alert, even when I was sitting still. Fear was a constant companion and I had learnt to hide it so that it would not be detected by anyone in my company. That in itself took a bit of work. I don't know why that has been the case. I imagine it was a coping mechanism that I developed as a child whenever I felt anxious. I have one particular memory that has always stayed with me. I was about eight years of age and the lunchtime bell had just rung at school. There was a lot of noise and the teacher told us that we weren't allowed to leave until everyone behaved. I knew that my father was waiting outside and I started to panic. I can clearly remember the physical sensations as I write. It took about ten minutes before we were allowed to leave, yet it felt like a lifetime. Deep down, I was afraid of being abandoned and that Dad would leave without me. It might sound irrational as he had never done this, yet it was a very real fear at the time. We all have core wounds and even if we never understand what triggered them, they are there. Abandonment is one that has been with me forever. Realizing this has helped me understand my behavior, particularly after my marriage ended, and it explains some of the unhealthy relationships I tolerated since. I am determined to no longer run my life from that place of fear. There were only disastrous consequences when I did. I have worked hard to heal and let go of old hurts, so much so that my dread of abandonment is almost nonexistent. Prompted by the words of my yoga teacher, I read up on the nervous system – the sympathetic nervous system (fight or flight) and the parasympathetic nervous system (rest and recovery) – how they work together and balance each other out. They are both part of a larger system called the Autonomic Nervous System. I think we're all familiar with our sympathetic nervous system, as modern day living calls on it a lot. Whether it is physical, psychological or environmental, we're assaulted at every turn and it can be hard to switch off. We all know the increased heart rate, tightening of muscles and release of adrenaline that accompanies a stressful day. Although this system plays a vital role in protecting us, it is meant to be a short-term measure. I had no idea how damaging it is to live in this mode for prolonged periods of time. It causes inflammation in the body and can lead to dis-ease. I had no knowledge of the parasympathetic nervous system either, and more importantly, how to activate it. It is basically our body's way of switching off the stress response and returning it to homeostasis. The Occupational Therapist I met as part of the cancer rehabilitation program also put a big emphasis on the stress and tiredness that comes from excessive mental activity. A constantly active mind is a real drain on our energy supply. Even though it may be invisible to others, it has a real impact on our health. She advised me to rest and recharge (mentally and physically) during the day. Like my yoga teacher, she reminded me that recharging is when mind and body are switched off and we activate the all-important parasympathetic nervous system. When I was on high alert all the time, I never considered the damage it was doing. I just assumed that I had naturally high levels of energy, which I did. However, I was depleting them by not properly recharging. Now looking back, I'm not the least bit surprised that cancer showed up in my body. It was almost inevitable. Our purpose or *why* for doing things is also key. We have all met busy people who are active, happy and engaged. They are full of energy because they are in the zone doing something they love. There are also busy people who are very stressed and unhappy. I have met both types of people, and I want to learn from those who live consciously, doing things that matter to them and feed them in some way. It has a very different impact on the body and can switch on the Parasympathetic Nervous System. When the fight or flight system is switched off, the body and mind can rest. I have no doubt that a combination of being constantly busy and not feeling nourished, definitely leads us down a road where self-care is nonexistent. We suffer greatly as a result.

I'd encourage you to check in and see if you are ever activating that important system in your body. I know that when I felt overwhelmed or exhausted, I turned to alcohol, stayed up late, and binged on TV. No judgment, but I wasn't getting in the zone where my body and mind could recharge. Most people have their poison when they feel overwhelmed, whether it is food, over-exercising, being glued to a phone or some other distraction. We feel we deserve it even though we know it is not a healthy solution in the long-term. When we are truly relaxed, our heart rate slows, our breathing calms. As we're not in fight or flight mode, blood goes to our organs rather than our muscles. It also helps us digest our food, we repair and we make hormones. All the research tells us that being in this mode regularly is essential for coping with life in a healthy way. As you would expect, activities like meditation, mindfulness, yoga, breathing exercises, Tai Chi, and gentle aerobic exercise are all recognized ways to activate the parasympathetic nervous system. In time, we come to know when it is switched on. I now do this through my own practices of meditation and breath work. I would encourage you to build some activity into your daily life that is just for you, something that allows you to slow down and refuels you.

If you feel objections rearing their head, like the old *I don't have time* chestnut, I'll share some words from Anita Moorjani that might change your mind:

The more you love yourself, the more positive energy you emanate, the less you love yourself, the less you emanate positive energy, and the more dependent you become on feeding off other people's energy.

Simply put, we uplift people when we are in a good place. When we sacrifice our well-being out of a sense of duty, we only end up draining those around us. We do more damage than good. Our self-care program is directly connected to our self-esteem levels. Do you believe that you are worth investing in and looking after? Whether it is food, exercise, rest, saying no, asking for help, carving out time just for you or positive self-talk, how you treat yourself is the true measure of your self-worth. Whatever it is that you want for your life, prioritizing your needs and feeling confident enough to voice them is half the battle. What better example to set for your family, friends and anyone who meets you. We definitely can't encourage others to take better care of themselves if we're not practicing it for ourselves.

Gift

Learning to look after myself and not just deprive or indulge myself gave me a healthy sense of self-respect. I know that how I treated myself was directly connected to my feelings of not being worthy. I have a new appreciation for my health (mind, body and spirit) and now am so much better equipped to deal with life.

Part III – Co-Creating Your Life

It took me a long time to understand that I could align with the power of intention and shape my life. We all have that capacity. Once I realized this, there was no going back. I could no longer live helplessly. I knew it was time to pick up the reins and take ownership of my life. I don't mean trying to control life. I'm talking about living from a deeper place. It is a spacious place where we move into a state of flow. It is the womb of creativity and possibility. We trust, we open our hearts, we set intention and we connect with that loving power. We stay present and watch what happens as life naturally unfolds. We can then respond and create. We take action as needed. Practicing this consistently has become an important discipline in my life. It is no longer just a once-off when the mood takes me or I'm feeling desperate. It is a new way of being in the world. I have been on this path for the last four years and it has been life-changing. Although I still get knocked off course and try to force life, very quickly the feeling of discomfort lets me know that I'm starting to derail. I suppose a lifetime of old habits takes time to rewire, so I'd encourage you to be kind and patient with yourself as you take these steps.

In the final chapter, I share a tool that I developed called *InsideOut Living*. It is designed to help you harness all your innate abilities and become a co-creator. We don't do this alone. We do it by working with the great intelligence that resides within. I didn't believe it possible until I tried it for myself. Everything changes when you learn to work with life rather than fighting it.

Chapter 22

An Intentional Life

By banishing doubt and trusting your intuitive feelings, you clear
a space for the power of intention to flow through.
Wayne Dyer

It might sound a bit odd to be talking about intention towards the end when really intention is where we start. Nevertheless, I think it is an important topic to explore before we step into the powerful position of co-creator. As I learn about it from teachers and ancient wisdom traditions, I see that it changes everything. It goes well beyond my capacity to fully understand, yet I get that when I tap into it, I can change my life immeasurably. Intention is connected with feelings of abundance and brings together many of the themes I have already explored. Intention changes our focus – from feelings of want to choice, from destination to direction, from living in the future to being present, from lack to contentedness, from discontent to acceptance and appreciation, from self-sabotage and limiting beliefs to trust and possibility. I see it as life force working through me, expressing who I am and my deepest desires. My intentions now come from aligning with that loving energy. Even in this short space of time, the right opportunities and situations have started to show up. I just know the next right action to take and where to focus my efforts. It works as long as I stay out of the way and don't block or try to force life. It works when I trust that what is next for me will naturally flow. It works as long as I allow and don't rush to create before the time is right. Looking back, I never lived from that place. I never had a clear intention or any intention really, other than to get through life. I felt I had been dealt my fair share of struggles and challenges, so I lived in the hope that I was due a break. I deserve it, is what I told myself. I mistakenly believed that I was a powerless victim and it is a miserable way to live. I had no intention, at least no conscious intention, which was worse. Being unconscious meant I was creating situations and experiences that weren't necessarily what I wanted. So without conscious clear intention, what could I really expect?

I see intention-setting as very different to goal-setting. Ideally they work together. I didn't consider intentions – well, seriously anyway – and I rarely set goals. Intention really is the *why* or motivation behind our goals. It is an inner exercise of tapping into our power center. Goal-setting is outward, action-oriented, and achieving them is often beyond our control. Setting goals without a clear intention is likely to lead to disappointment. If we have a clear intention and even if we don't succeed in that particular goal, we trust that whatever comes along is lined up with our intention and is for our highest good. I will give you one example of how this has unfolded for me. After cancer, I could see that there was an opportunity for me to move onto a new path or just return to my old life. (I'm not sure that was ever going to be a possibility as I had changed so much.) I really felt like I was standing at a crossroads and the decisions that I made would determine how the next phase of my life turned out. I had never been a goal-oriented person in my life. Goal-setting always sounded quite cold and calculated to me. I associated it with business, competition and struggle. It just wasn't part of my vernacular. The first thing that became clear to me was that under no circumstance could I go back to the life I had been living. All well and good, but what did I want? I didn't have a clear picture. I just knew that I wanted a simpler, more connected way of life that had meaning. Over time a clear intention did start to make itself known. I now had a roadmap and tools for living well. I had the experience of healing my life. I knew that my personal struggles had to serve some greater purpose. I felt a powerful connection to my life source that nothing could quench. I imagined that I might have something of value to share with others who were struggling like I had struggled. I was conscious that I must be the living example of what I was learning. I must walk my talk. I still slip and fall regularly, yet I know that is just part and parcel of life.

So my high-level intention became: *I want to live as the fullest expression of myself and use my life experience and skills to be of service in the world.* Now more than ever, the planet needs us to step into the fullness of who we are and express our unique gifts. In my book, it is the key to a long, healthy life. Dr. Martin Luther King said of service: *Everybody can be great because everybody can serve...*

That was it. Not a specific list of things that I was going to do, but more like a theme tune to my life, whatever I ended up doing. It was my starting point, and with that intended starting point, going back to my old life was no longer an option. From that intention came the decision to train as a life coach, to write this book, to meditate daily, to learn from great teachers and mentors, to surround myself with like-minded people who encourage me to stretch myself, and many more decisions. Everything I now practice on a daily basis is lined up with this intention. I slip and have days where I go totally off track and that's okay. For example, writing this book was never a goal of mine initially, yet once I had a clear intention for my life, the book just happened. I heeded the signs and I was getting many of them. Once it started to take shape, it became my goal to finish it and get it published. I also had to take action. I sat down every day and wrote, even if it was just a few lines. I knew I needed to maintain a momentum if I was to complete it. I made hundreds of submissions to publishers all over the world until I was successful in getting a contract. Intention meets goal and action. Intention without focus and action can end up just as pipe dreams that never materialize. Goals without conscious intention are likely just satisfying some ego desire. Moreover, when our goals and actions are not lined up with a conscious intention, there is often conflict and likely disappointment.

Deepak Chopra, in his book *The Seven Spiritual Laws of Success*, explains the law of intention and desire. *Our intentions and desires, when released in the field of pure potentiality, have infinite organizing power.* He goes on to explain that inherent in every desire are the mechanics for its fulfillment. This isn't a mystical notion. For example, when we have a desire to walk, our intention

> *incites millions of chemical reactions and electrical impulses that obey fixed laws of nature... at the level of pure consciousness, there is nothing other than energy and information... we can consciously change the energy and information of our own body, and influence the energy and information of our extended body – our environment – and cause things to manifest in it.*

He points out that intention is the real power behind desire because intention is desire without attachment to the outcome – not an easy one. We set the intention and then let go. It doesn't mean we just sit back and do nothing. Instead we take action that supports our intentions. We act, believe and feel as if it has happened, not necessarily knowing when or how it will come to fruition. If we focus only on the outcome, we are focused on the future and can miss out on opportunities that show up along the way. We might not see the full picture. We may not see that our desire is being fulfilled, as it might unfold differently to how we imagined. It isn't easy. I have to keep reminding myself to let go, stay present and just deal with what is right in front of me. Mindfulness is really helpful here as it keeps us in the moment and not in the future where we want to see our goals fulfilled. We can only take action towards our intention in the present. It is the only place where change can happen. It is where we align with creative energy. That is authentic power. Yesterday and tomorrow are only ideas. When I start speculating on the future, I start imagining everything that might go wrong. I see an outcome that I don't want and a multitude of problems show up. I am putting the cart before the horse when I focus on the end goal rather than living and creating in the now. Deepak Chopra explains that it is through our attention and intention that we bring about change.

Attention energizes and intention transforms. Whatever we put our attention on grows stronger in our life... Intention triggers the transformation of energy and information, and organizes its own fulfilment... we see the expression of this organizing power in every blade of grass, in every flower, in everything that is alive.

I am learning in real time as I write this chapter. I have talked about training as a life coach, writing this book, putting healthy, supportive practices in place and I'm proud that I have come so far. I have an intention for my life, yet I have no idea what the future holds. I have a direction and I am committed to this direction. There are plenty of times when I drift into the future. I worry and imagine everything that might go wrong, like not making a living or being proved wrong by naysayers. You get the picture. We are all faced with situations like this every day. We convince ourselves that if we mentally consider all the possible things that could go wrong, we will be better prepared for what might happen. We put our attention on the wrong things, forgetting that what we think about and focus on expands. We give our energy to worries and fears, and so they grow. We take our focus off the present and end up sabotaging ourselves as a result. It is too easy to put it down to being unlucky or jinxed when things don't work out the way we hope. Look at intention as like starting the engine. Things start connecting behind the scenes to get us moving. Our attention is then like the fuel that keeps us moving towards the fulfillment of our goals.

So why do we do this if there is another way? Why do we tie ourselves so tightly to an outcome that we are not responding naturally to life as it unfolds? From my experience it is because of fear and a need to control. I don't want my soft spots triggered as it will cause me emotional pain. I don't want to upset my apple cart, and in my effort to control everything around me, I get stuck and use up a lot of energy. Have you ever heard someone describe a dream that is subject to a lot of conditions? It must happen within a specific timeframe or manifest in a particular way. I know I often did this and gave up on my goal as a result. For example, I'm sure we all know someone, or maybe that person who would like to find love in their life. Because of past letdowns, you might have a list of conditions – they must look a certain way, earn a certain income, have certain interests and on and on. Before you even meet the person, your need to control will likely prevent it from ever happening.

Michael Singer, in his book *The Untethered Soul*, explains this tendency in a chapter called *Removing Your Inner Thorn*. The inner thorn represents emotional sensitivities or inner disturbances that we want to protect ourselves from feeling. He uses the analogy of having a thorn stuck in your arm. It is painful and it disturbs you so much when the thorn is touched that you need to make sure nothing does. It creates a problem for you as it makes it hard to get close to people. He suggests another way. Take the thorn out. Feel the pain. Once you do that, there is no need to prevent people from getting too close. You are free. He illustrates very clearly how the choices we make with our own inner thorns have a profound impact on the course of our lives. Take the thorn of loneliness and rejection as an example. We make the choice to keep these thorns. If we're lonely we might avoid going to places or situations where we will be surrounded by couples. If we're afraid of being rejected, we will avoid getting too close to people. We will do whatever it takes to avoid triggering those feelings. We end up adjusting our life to make allowances for our thorns. We limit our lives. All of these thorns are blocked energies, often there since childhood. He shows us that it is possible to release them.

I cannot do justice to Michael Singer's book, but I feel drawn to touch on some points that have helped me. He clearly explains how to remove our inner thorns. We learn to become the observer of our thoughts and feelings. We stay in neutral awareness. We get off the pitch (field) and watch the match from the sidelines. We realize that we are not our thoughts because we can observe them as they come and go. Yet we don't come and go. We create space and ultimately see that we are not what we think and feel. This might sound like a strange concept, but if you are ready, you can develop some practices that allow you to separate yourself from the noise. You will realize that it is always passing and more noise will keep replacing it. Thoughts and feelings will continue to come and go and you are still here. I cannot say that I have mastered the art, but I have gotten glimpses of total stillness, peace and joy. It is beyond description. A desire has been born in me to spend more time in this state and to live in a more peaceful and fluid manner. This is the key to setting intentions. If we are trying to protect a lot of inner thorns, our intentions become clouded and often in conflict with our thoughts and actions. That is why we get stuck or derailed. We then blame it on outside forces or not being good enough. In Michael Singer's example, the underlying intention is to find love. In this case, if your fear of rejection stops you from taking any risks or allowing someone get close to you, then your thorns are negatively impacting your life. If you do get close to someone, you will be watching what you say and do so as to avoid rejection. But there is a way out of this vicious cycle. I learnt a few home truths from reading that.

I struggled with my inner thorns for a long time. I suppressed so much, trying to ensure nothing triggered pain inside. I genuinely didn't know there was a possibility of being free of them. I thought it was my lot for life. Visiting Pádraig the healer was the catalyst for letting go. I felt an oceanful of pain being released. Now I feel like I have space inside and I'm not afraid of sitting quietly with myself. When things do happen that upset me, I know what I need to do.

- I take a few deep breaths.
- I focus my attention on my heart center and visualize an image of it. It might be a bright light, a flower, a color. Focus on whatever image comes to you.
- I picture this center opening and radiating light out into the world.
- Then I ask any emotion that is stuck to come to the surface.
- I acknowledge it with love and I let the energy move through me.

This is a simple practice. Sometimes there is discomfort or tears, but it passes. Sometimes it happens quickly and at other times I have to sit a bit longer. It depends on how big the thorn is and how long it has been stuck inside. I also use breath work, journaling, movement and other practices to support me.

You must look inside yourself and determine that from now on pain is not a problem… It's a thing in the universe that is passing through your system.
Michael Singer

His words really registered with me. We only suffer long-term emotional pain when we continually suppress how we feel. I can definitely vouch for that. When we allow ourselves to fully feel an emotion in all its intensity, we honor our experiences. We process the emotion and then it just leaves our system. I believe it would be a great step forward if *emotional health* was a subject on the school curriculum. It might help remove the stigma that still lingers around the subject. I don't mean teaching techniques to bypass how we feel. I mean teaching the importance of acknowledging our emotions and the tools to release them safely. Emotions are just a natural part and parcel of being a healthy human being. They show us that we are truly alive. When we do this, we are free to work with the life force that can then flow freely through us. Anxiety might be a thing of the past if we could master that one.

Intention really is a powerful force in our lives. I have set an intention for my life. I also set intentions for my year, my month and my day. It is almost automatic now as I have gotten into the habit of going about my day consciously. I'm not rigid about it as life is constantly in motion, but I have practices that I use to keep me focused and on track. I know what works for me now. First thing in the morning I meditate. I sit quietly and release whatever intention comes into the universe. Sometimes it can just be as simple as focusing on gratitude for the day. I journal most mornings or evenings and often my intention may come out on the page. I then hand it over, trusting that whatever is meant to happen will happen. I try to stay present during the day and take actions that support my intention. This helps me get clarity.

Setting intentions is co-creating at its best. The more we are in harmony with the field of intention, the more we are able to do all that this field of intention is able to do. We can heal, attract abundance and the right people show up at the right time. What is your intention for your life, your day, your work? Maybe it is time to really tune in and merge with the heartbeat of your life.

Gift

Learning about the power of intention has brought a great momentum to my life. I have a north star which is now my guiding force. It has brought me great joy and a sense of purpose that I never felt before.

Chapter 23

A New Age, A New Kind Of Human

We are witnessing an enormous shift of collective consciousness throughout the world. We are at the precipice of great transformation within our culture and government.
Zachary Quinto

There can be little doubt that evolution on planet earth is taking a big leap forward. Events in 2020 rocked many of us to the core, yet the signs had long been there that life as we knew it was no longer working. The collective shift in consciousness that started long before the arrival of COVID-19 had already stimulated many of us to rethink the way we live, what is important to us, and who we want to be in the world. When I started writing this book over three years ago, the old world order was already breaking down. Life as I was living it had definitely stopped working and it took a cancer diagnosis for me to hit the reset button. As a collective, we too have been getting wake-up call after wake-up call. We have seen endless revelations of abuse and corruption around the world, and as I write this, I suspect there is more yet to come. Political upheaval and social unrest have become the norm. Overpopulation, pollution and reliance on nonrenewable resources have left our environment screaming *no more*. The red flags were there. Our way of life was no longer sustainable. In Ireland, increasing problems with homelessness and a healthcare system that was on its knees had us wondering where it had all gone so wrong. Financial prosperity hadn't necessarily translated into better lives for most. Stress and anxiety were rife and many were struggling just to make ends meet. Endless consumption, hailed as a panacea for our discontent, was no longer tenable or appealing for many, including me. The penny was definitely beginning to drop. We needed a planetary reboot, a time to reprioritize.

As we have seen, this wake-up call is painful. It is chaotic and turbulent. We are letting go of the old without knowing what lies ahead. I found my own wake-up call with cancer very challenging. My world as I knew it just dissolved in front of my eyes as I was brought to a standstill. I watched life go on as normal while inside I was lost. I had no idea what lay ahead and there was no going back. It felt like the ground had disappeared from under my feet. It is now only four years later that I'm starting to emerge into the world as a different person. It takes time to birth the new. So too on the planet we are purging the old so that we can create the new. The underbelly and all its ugliness is being revealed, and although traumatic, I believe it is necessary. As with our personal challenges, we can only heal what we see and feel. We must acknowledge the dark before it can be transmuted into light. We are being freed of the fear that comes from being controlled and dominated for a very long time. In Ireland, there have already been many changes for the better. Looking back at the dark periods in our history, it feels like we are finally entering the light. We are shaking off and healing the residue left from famine, colonization, abuse, inequality and poverty; letting go of our inherited trauma so we can create anew.

It starts with us as individuals. We have reached the time for reclaiming our power and birthing a new kind of human. This human is a co-creator. They are aligned with universal intelligence and understand the unlimited nature of their true potential. Their heart is open. They are expressing their unique creative gifts both for their own well-being and for the sake of the world. They are shaping their individual future and are part of shaping the future of the collective. In Abraham Maslow's hierarchy of needs, this person has reached the top of the triangle (self-transcendence). For many of us there is a way to go yet. Maslow stated that in modern society people are generally stuck between survival needs and growth needs, ultimately a damaging state long-term. They have not found a vocation or purposeful career. *If the essential core of the person is denied or suppressed, he gets sick sometimes in obvious ways, sometimes in subtle ways, sometimes immediately, sometimes later.* I believe we have been given the time to reflect, recalibrate and participate in setting a new course for our lives. From my own experience, the only way to do this is to go within. When I live in harmony with a deeper reality, I am open to receiving the wisdom and answers that the universe has to offer. From this stillness, I can then have a positive impact in the world. Understanding this has changed me beyond recognition. I have a new lease of life that I never expected. I feel more creative, connected and supported than ever. It is hard to articulate other than to say that I feel like I have been reborn as my true self. There is a beautiful simplicity to my life that was never there before. Maslow says – *The great lesson from the true mystics is that the sacred is in the ordinary, that it is found in one's daily life, in one's neighbors, friends, and family.* That was definitely brought home to me during lockdown. Simple tasks that I would have put little value on in the past took on a whole new meaning. I started doing the weekly grocery shopping for my mother and an elderly neighbor. I know that's no major feat, and for many of you, particularly those with large families, grocery shopping may be the bane of your life. However, as a single person it was not my life. Now here I was doing something small to help someone else, and no matter how small, it felt good to be of service. I was being reminded of what is truly important. I'm fairly sure that when I'm lying on my deathbed, I won't be reflecting on all the running around that I did. I will return to the loving connections I made, the lives that I touched and those that touched mine. This is just one example. I could list many more. During this time I also realized that all my needs are met. Right now I may have less materially than I ever did, yet I have so much more in other ways. I wouldn't change a thing. I know for sure that the path to a contented life is not found in things. It is just not possible to find lasting contentment in the impermanent. I feel like I am plugged in for the first time. I'm a novice and at the early stages of the learning curve. I get plenty of wobbles. I go off track. I revert to old patterns. They are just a reminder that I have disconnected and need to get back in balance. It's a lifelong journey for me now. I sit, find my breath, meditate, get out in nature or write. In essence, I need solitude. My exploration started as a way to escape my agitated mind but soon became a way to merge with the sacred still place. Thom Hartmann in his book, *The Last Hours of Ancient Sunlight*, describes the true power of meditation:

> *The true reason for meditating is to become awake in this very moment. And from that place – that here-and-now touching of the power of life – we can find the ability to transform ourselves and others in ways which can and will transform the world.*

I have found a path that has meaning for me. I'm starting out and I have no choice but to follow it, wherever it leads. I know it is the only way that I will have true peace and feel whole. My practice is my way of staying centered in my daily life. There are many different methods and I'd encourage you to experiment and find what works for you. It's the one destination regardless of how you find it. Be patient and have compassion when you struggle. It took the bombshell of cancer for me to finally pay attention. I had to break down before I could see that it really was a breakthrough. Life was giving me an opportunity. It is not always easy to put the brakes on. Modern life is fast and we are being mentally bombarded all the time. In the words of Mooji – *Everyone is suffering from a lack of inner space.* We were taught to revere the intellect and equate busyness with a sense of worth. Our mind is a wonderful tool, it is just not meant to be our master. We are not the voice in our heads and the fact that we can observe it demonstrates this. *Come to know the one who watches the voice, and you will come to know one of the great mysteries of creation,* says Michael Singer in *The Untethered Soul.* I know it's time to rein it in when I get lost in a train of negative thought. I'm disappearing down the rabbit hole and the only way I can get back on track is through my practice. When I'm connected and in flow, ideas and decisions come easily and I put them in to action with little effort. In this mode, my life is more spontaneous and fun. I had spent a lot of time overanalyzing and anxious, to the point that I was almost paralyzed. When I am able to become still, life is easier. I accomplish more in the end. Oprah Winfrey says it perfectly – *It is from the still place that you create your best life.* It is from the still place that I wrote this book. I couldn't have done it otherwise. Our time in lockdown was surely giving us the opportunity to experience the still place. It is always available to us. It is only ever a breath away.

So why do we give our power away? Why haven't we been encouraged to be self-reliant, resourceful and the masters of our own destiny? Why is this not a part of our educational curriculum? What industry or business will thrive if people live fully in their power? Who benefits when we feel whole, capable, healthy and connected to our inner wisdom? Who benefits when we are not limited by our beliefs, when we feel empowered and confident in our decisions? Who wants us to know that we have everything we need within to live a fulfilling life? I can think of many institutions that benefit when we live in fear and are disempowered – the pharmaceutical industry, banks, governments, churches and many more. As long as we live in fear, we can be controlled. We can be saved. We can be manipulated. When I was training as a coach, the term *white coat syndrome* was used to explain how we give away our power. This can take many forms and happens in many situations. We may not even be aware that we are doing it. Instead, we register it afterwards when we feel exploited, impotent or resentful. The term *white coat*, I imagine, was coined from the doctor-patient relationship. It is not meant to be a criticism of the profession as they are doing what they know best. It just typifies how we often hand over responsibility for our lives to others. I spent a lot of time looking to others for validation and answers, believing that I was small and inadequate. I knew nothing about stepping into my power.

The fact is, we are very powerful beings and each of us has something special to offer the world. Now is a critical time for discovering our unique form of self-expression and owning it. It is time to turn our light on. It is through our differences that we will unite and celebrate our diversity. We can then play our individual roles in whatever systems we are a part of, whether it be family, work, friendships, organizations or communities. I see this as the new human in action; each of us embracing who we are and being of service to the greater good. I know from personal experience that great stress is caused when we ignore the deep creative calling that goes beyond time and space. When we honor our vocation and are true to ourselves, we really blossom. We are here to have experiences that help us grow, expand and awaken to who we really are. Long before cancer I knew the sands were shifting and I was changing inside. There was nothing I could do to stop it, even if I had wanted to. I had outgrown my life as it was and I was nudged, and eventually pushed, into the next stage. I just didn't know what that looked like, so I ended up stuck and rigid with fear. I had stopped trusting myself a long time before. Painful experiences had caused me to shut down. I felt like I was suffocating because I had no creative outlet. I really felt like I was dying inside. I was resentful of those who were expressing themselves creatively. Now I can see that they were being a mirror for me. They were there to help me wake up, but I couldn't see it at the time. Instead

I closed myself off and kept moving and doing on the hamster wheel. It took a long time for me to realize that much of it was of my own making. When I came across the book, *The Hamster Wheel is Not Motorized,* by Benjamin Ramakrishna, I had a flash of insight. I was doing it to myself. I didn't know there was another way. I love this quote from American author Richard Bach – *Argue for your limitations and sure enough they're yours.* Yet we do it all the time. I did it over and over again. When I read his words I knew it was an insane way to live. Defending beliefs that limit us only closes us off from many great possibilities. Limiting beliefs come from a place of fear. I was full of fear before I got sick. I was afraid of being judged and rejected and the list goes on. Then I was diagnosed with breast cancer which was worse than anything I had feared, and when it happened I had no fear. I was able to handle it. I was stronger than I ever thought I was. There is nothing to fear. We rarely experience the future we fear, unless we wish it into existence. The same holds true for our emotional state. Nobody can make us feel a certain way – how we feel is a product of the choices we make. We do these things to ourselves. I had to learn that the hard way. My default position was to get frustrated and irritated when something didn't work out the way I thought it should. It could have been sitting in traffic and getting angry with the driver in front of me, or having a difference of opinion with someone at work and believing they were out to get me. In every moment we make a choice. We are not prisoners or victims in our lives. We have the power to determine how our life turns out just by how we think and feel. I was constantly fighting with life. I shifted my attitude and now choose to look at life as happening *for* me, not *to* me. It's not always easy. Still, I know it is the truth and it has completely changed how I experience life.

Paraphrasing Wayne Dyer:

You are responsible for your thoughts – you can control your thoughts, if they are immobilizing you, why would you defend them? If you believe it is human nature or in your genes, then you're stuck. You can't change, you can't grow. Feelings come from thoughts. Emotions are the result of the things that you think in your life. If they don't work, stop defending them. Get rid of them. Stop expecting the world to be something it isn't or people to be something they are not. Stop fighting.

I have heard times of great change being described like a pendulum swinging from left to right before finding a new balance. This seems to be the case in the world now. There are polarized opinions on every topic and little tolerance of difference. Hateful discourse is not unusual, particularly on social media. Maybe this is part and parcel of getting over the past. Like a caged animal going a bit crazy when it is freed, we too are exorcising our own demons for a time. I often judged others. I was insecure and unhappy in my life and it was easier to lash out than face the battle going on inside. I believe that we will find a new balance. We will recognize that we are all part of one living, breathing organism and need each other for survival. We are just different spokes on the wheel. Ram Dass, American spiritual teacher, psychologist and author said, *Treat everyone you meet like God in drag.* We come from the one source consciousness and we are just different expressions of it. We are wearing different costumes. When we wake up to this truth, we won't have any desire to criticize each other any longer. We will want to celebrate and enjoy what makes each of us unique.

There are many new organizations and communities emerging every day, bringing together groups of people with common visions and ideas for the next stage of our evolution. I'll mention two of them here, and there are so many more that have emerged since I started writing. Thrive Global and the HeartMath Institute sparked my interest. I am always on the lookout for new communities and movements that are about transformation and conscious evolution. I want to be part of the work that they are doing.

Thrive Global was founded by Arianna Huffington, co-founder of the *Huffington Post* – www.thriveglobal.com.

Its mission is:

> *to end the stress and burnout epidemic by offering companies and individuals sustainable, science-based solutions to enhance well-being, performance, and purpose, and create a healthier relationship with technology. Recent science has shown that the pervasive belief that burnout is the price we must pay for success is a delusion. We know, instead, that when we prioritize our well-being, our decision-making, creativity, and productivity improve dramatically. Thrive Global is committed to accelerating the culture shift that allows people to reclaim their lives and move from merely surviving to thriving.*

It is an excellent resource, featuring great articles and information. I referred to her book *Thrive* earlier and I highly recommend it.

The HeartMath Institute is a nonprofit research and education institute. Its vision is to help individuals, organizations, and the global community, incorporate the heart's intelligence into their day-to-day experience of life – www.heartmath.org.

> *HeartMath shows us a way to remake our world. It provides tools to connect with our inner guidance and technologies to help us be still enough to listen. Its research shows us how we can be empowered to become masters of ourselves and the quality of our future. Together, the tools, technologies and research enable us to realize our full potential as individuals and as a species to serve as caretakers for our planet and generations to come.*

Rollin McCraty, researcher with the HeartMath Institute,

explains in his article "The Energetic Heart" that:

the heart generates the largest electromagnetic field in the body. The electrical field as measured in an electrocardiogram (ECG) is about 60 times greater in amplitude than the brain waves recorded in an electroencephalogram (EEG).

He goes on to explain how this knowledge has implications for the inner dynamics of health, disease and our interactions with others. Living from the heart is not just an expression, it is a necessity.

Like my experience with cancer, there is no going back. I believe the old world is gone and we have no choice but to find sustainable and harmonious ways of being at one with each other and our planet. Everything I have experienced has definitely caused me to question what progress means for me personally. It is clear to me that the epidemics of cancer, anxiety and mental illness are the price we have paid collectively in the name of progress. We prioritized economic progress and put profit before people. The Oxfam International "Time to Care" Report, published in January 2020, is full of staggering statistics that make for grim reading:

Economic inequality is out of control. In 2019, the world's billionaires, only 2,153 people, had more wealth than 4.6 billion people. This great divide is based on a flawed and sexist economic system that values the wealth of the privileged few, mostly men, more than the billions of hours of the most essential work – the unpaid and underpaid care work done primarily by women and girls around the world.

Now we have an opportunity to reprioritize and let social progress and community be our guiding light. We may understand that a stressed system is at the root of our imbalance, but it isn't always easy to remedy. Being present is an essential quality for mental wellness, Abraham Maslow tells us. The turbulent times of 2020 gave us all an opportunity to become still and present as we were confined indoors for many months. Only time will tell what we have learnt from that period in confinement.

The question is – *Are we going to seize the opportunity that is in front of us? Are we ready to evolve consciously with a shared vision for life on planet earth?* I believe we will. Although it may take time, I think it is going to change us beyond recognition and for the better. I believe we will do this by coming together as new kind of humans who are not afraid of their real power.

Gift

There have been many. I am now expressing myself creatively and I know that when I'm plugged in my true potential is unlimited. When I lived from my ego mind I was never satisfied. I felt small, constricted and afraid. I was disconnected from my power source. I thought *more* was the solution and yet it was *never* enough. Now, on my good days I am connected to that place of harmony and flow. I am home.

Chapter 24

InsideOut Living

We're living in an age of high stress and fear, and in the midst of trying to protect ourselves from everything we think is "out there," we've forgotten to enjoy ourselves and to take care of what's inside.
Anita Moorjani

In this final chapter, I introduce a toolkit that I developed as I was learning new ways to navigate life. Once I understood that real, lasting change only happened when I focused on me, and not the world around me, I knew this was the place to start. Now it is where I find my answers and the energy to live authentically. Whether we know it or not, we are all active participants in how our life plays out. We are powerful co-creators. When you really grasp this fact you will live your life wholeheartedly. You will feel excited by life and you will get great clarity on who you are and how you want to show up. It took the shock of breast cancer for me to fully engage with life in this way. I know I keep saying it, but cancer really was a rebirth for me in every sense of the word. I would not be where I am today if it hadn't pulled the plug and stopped me in my tracks. My life had felt like a straitjacket and the societal emphasis on materialism and individualism held no meaning for me anymore. The intervening years have infused my life with a deeper sense of purpose. Life definitely works better for me when I move with it rather than fighting against it. When we synchronize with the life force that animates all things, we move with a sense of ease and flow that is felt in every cell of our bodies. It becomes our guiding light.

I call this exercise the *InsideOut Living Indicator* as it is about directing your energy inwards to the aspects of your life that only you can determine. When you are hooked up to your power source you will instinctively know what to do. Is your belief system supporting you? Have you healthy boundaries? Do you nurture your relationship with yourself? Are you trusting life rather than resisting it? These are just some of the questions you might consider as you go through the exercise. At some point we have all convinced ourselves that the external world is where our solutions lie. We believe that if others changed or we had more money or possessions, life would be great. *They* are not the answer. *We* are always our own answer. Nice things may be a nice by-product, but in and of themselves they do not lead to a sustained contentment. Expecting others to change is a futile exercise and not really our business. Everyone lives according to their own truth and their life circumstances. We can also live helplessly, reacting to whatever life throws at us. That is a depressing way to live. I have been there and it brought me nothing but misery. There is a better way. Echoing the words of Anita Moorjani, living with stress and fear has caused us to neglect our inner world. We must go within. It is the only place I could find the deeper meaning I always craved. It was only when cancer knocked on my door that I felt like I had finally been handed the instruction book for life.

Preparation

Before starting the exercise, I will remind you of the vision for your life that you created in Chapter 19. I suggest that you have it written down in front of you before getting to work. This is an opportunity to check in and see if your inner life is aligned with your personal dreams. You are going to hit some resistance and blocks along the way if they are not in harmony with each other. I would also suggest that you consider the part that you want to play in the next stage of the planet's evolution. It is up to each of us to focus on the lessons from this challenging and exciting period of our history. How will we reemerge and rebuild our world? What are your dreams for our global community? We are all here to honor our soul's calling, but we are also here to be of service to humanity and planet earth. We are essential pieces of the puzzle and taking time to reflect acts as a streamlining process. We get clarity on where to focus our energy. We get our ducks in a row. I'll briefly share some of my hopes for the future. They are broad-brush and aspirational. COVID-19 was a good reminder that none of us know what lies ahead. However, we can start to envision the future. It is only when we focus our energy on what we want to create that we can hope to make it happen.

My vision

- We are all awake and living consciously. We realize that we are not separate entities but individual expressions of the one. We embrace a universal spirituality that is about peace, self-realization, community and co-creation. As a result it makes no sense to judge or harm each other or the environment. Diversity is celebrated not judged. We create and work harmoniously in communities that share our interests and creative passions. We are driven by the desire to create a better life for all.

- Our work allows us to express ourselves creatively and reach our highest potential. Our education system is less about rote learning and more about helping each child uncover their unique gifts. We recognize that everyone has an important role to play in the world and our system is designed to connect children with the people and training they need to cultivate their gifts. The school curriculum is based on the needs of the world and creating meaningful work that is matched with the talents of the student.

- We live in an equitable society where the emphasis is on sustainability and purpose-oriented work that provides a living for all. Wealth is distributed so that everyone has a basic standard of living. There is free access to healthcare and education. The desires of the individual are harmonized with the needs of the collective. We are free to express our life purpose in creative work.

- Our health system focuses on the whole person (mind, body, spirit) and we understand how inextricably connected they are. The system encourages personal responsibility and acknowledges our powers for self-healing. We use the best of modern medicine combined with Eastern wisdom. Meditation, visualization, emotional release, exercise and diet are just some of the new ways that we treat and support total well-being of the mind and body. Understanding and working with our energy body will be paramount. Deepak Chopra says – *Medicine in the future will give everyone the ability to become their own best healer.*

- Our media upholds the positive vision that we have for the world and is not constantly churning out messages of fear and doom. We are constantly reminded of our successes and possibilities. We move out of the rigidity of fear and are inspired to create the new. That is true power. A positive momentum is being created that will keep us all working towards our shared vision for the planet.

The InsideOut Living Indicator

Take some time to reflect on each of the areas below. There are ten in total to consider. I have included some questions to help you. When you have done this, consider, on a scale of 1 to 10, how satisfied you are with each aspect of your life. 10 stands for very satisfied, and 1 for very dissatisfied. (10 is the outer line of the circle and 1 is at the center.) When you have decided on a number, mark it in the relevant section of the wheel. Then draw a line in each section depending on the score you have picked and connect them up to form a wheel (e.g. 5 means you will mark a line halfway through this section). I have included a blank wheel and a completed one to illustrate what I mean. When the lines have been connected you will see what your wheel looks like today. Obviously, the ideal wheel is when all elements are scored a 10, but the real purpose of the exercise is to look at the reality of where you are now and what aspects of your life need addressing. Awareness is the first powerful step we take on the road to change. For many years I was asleep. I didn't know that I could consciously influence the course of my life. Now I have tools to support me and when I get off balance I know how to re-center and get back on track.

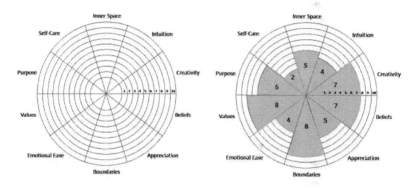

Inner space

This is how you connect with your power source. It is where you find your center of gravity again. Everything in life stems from this still space. It is your true nature. It is a field of infinite possibilities. When you are established in your awareness rather than the jumble of your thoughts, you realize that you have no boundaries. You are more expansive than you could have ever imagined. This is the womb of creativity. This is your engine house. Inspiration arises here. Your best decisions come from here. This is the place where you ground yourself and connect with your highest wisdom. Do you make time for silence or meditation? Do you have a practice for getting in touch with this loving, intelligent force that only wants the best for you?

Intuition

In-Tuition. This is the voice of your soul. This wise voice will come to life when you have spent time cultivating inner space. Your intuitive voice is soft and encouraging. The ego mind is the critical and judgmental voice that we are all too familiar with, as it harasses us on a daily basis. Intuition is a function of the heart not the mind and we now know that the electromagnetic field of the heart is sixty times more powerful than that of the mind (www.heartmath.org). Get to know the difference and tune into the supportive voice. It will guide you every step of the way. Do you trust your instincts? Do you listen to that gentle voice? Do you heed the nudges that you get? Are you living authentically? Once you become familiar with this voice and surrender to it, you will always be safe and on track.

Creativity

Unless you create you are unfulfilled, so says *A Course in Miracles.* How do you share your soul with the world? What makes your heart sing? Are you expressing yourself in a meaningful way? Are there times in your day when you feel in flow? What are you doing in these moments? Do you have any creative outlet in your life? Do you have fun? Do you take time out to play? Have you ever tried journaling to get your creative juices flowing? This is why we are here; to express what makes us unique. It is what brings us to life.

Beliefs

Have you ever observed the incessant, chattering voice that is narrating your every waking moment? Is it constructive and helpful? Is it running the show or are you? Do you have a set of empowering beliefs that support you? Or are there outdated programs still running that have no place in your life anymore? Can you identify limiting beliefs that are holding you back? Be honest. One of your limiting beliefs might be that you can't change, that you just are the way you are. If you believe that, you're stuck for sure. A belief is only a thought that you *keep* thinking. It is possible to change. Just think back on your life. It's unlikely you believe exactly what you did ten or fifteen years ago.

Appreciation

True power comes from *feeling* grateful. When you think of anything you are grateful for, stop. Really feel into it and what it adds to your life. Trust me. It will change how you feel. Gratitude changes your body chemistry, your energetic signature and your point of attraction. In his podcast, Daily Breath, Deepak Chopra, MD tells us that gratitude decreases inflammation in the body. Do you genuinely appreciate the good things in your life? Or do you hold a cynical view and compare yourself to others? It's okay if you do. No criticism. I've been there. Recognizing that it is only damaging *you* is the first step. Did you know that gratitude has the power to radically alter your experience of life? It will change how you behave in the moment, and it is only in the moment that we have the power to create our life.

Boundaries

Healthy boundaries indicate a healthy level of self-esteem. They are guiding principles for navigating relationships and feeling safe. We all have different limits and know what feels comfortable for us or not. Our boundaries communicate that to the world around us. We don't have to explain them. Check in with how you are feeling. Trust your senses. Trust your gut. Can you recognize when your boundaries have been compromised? Do you feel that your needs are as important as others? Can you say *No*, without worrying about the response you will get? Do you know how to protect your time and energy? Are you able to ask for what you need in a relationship?

Emotional Ease

We have healthy relationships when we take responsibility for our emotional pain rather than projecting it on to others. It is only when we look after our side of the street and what triggers us emotionally, that we can have fully functioning relationships. Dysfunction arises when we act out of unresolved traumas that we have not healed. Have you dealt with your childhood wounds? Can you feel your emotions and move on? Do you recognize when you are reacting from a place of pain? Have you healthy coping mechanisms when things go wrong? Are you a *point the finger* person or do you take personal responsibility? Whenever I feel triggered, I know it is time to address some unresolved emotion that still has a hold on me. I have to do the work.

Values

Your values help you get clear on your boundaries. What do you value most? What are your non-negotiables? What are your guiding principles? Are you clear on them? Are they aligned with your dreams? Are you aware of the cost when you dishonor yourself and compromise on your values? A boundary usually has been crossed. Do your values drive your decisions? A good way to check in is to ask the question – Which choice will bring me more peace? Trust what resonates. Our energetic resonance is our true GPS, not our thoughts.

Purpose

What is your *Why*? In wisdom traditions, the concept of dharma (cosmic law and order in Eastern traditions) includes our purpose. One aspect is dharma as our path in life. Wayne Dyer describes our dharma as, *what we are here to be, not do.* Who are you being in every moment of your life? Are you honoring your calling? What gets you out of bed every morning other than the alarm clock? Do you feel that you have something to contribute to the world? Do you believe you can make a difference? Are you living in a way that is connected with your values? What is the expertise that life has given you that you can use to help others? What is your life experience telling you about your gifts?

Self-Care

Do you exercise and eat food that nourishes you? Do you get support if you have a problem? Are there people in your life who are positive and uplifting? Do you block out periods of time that are just for you? Is there a balance of give and take in your life? Do you pay attention when your body is telling you that it needs some love? Do you treat yourself as you would a good friend or a child that is dear to you? Have you a community of like-minded people that you can check in with for advice or mentoring? This can be online or in person, but it is important to have people around you who get you and add something to your life.

What your score is telling you:

The assessment below is designed to give you a broad indication of what your score is telling you. It will hopefully provide some material for reflection. Talking it through one-to-one can help you delve further into the results. Powerful insights and healing arise when we are willing to dig deep. We end up living from a very authentic place and feel grounded in who we are. There is very little that can knock us off track as we have hooked up to a very reliable guidance system that has only our best interests at heart. Once you have a desire to change and are committed to a new way of relating to life, nothing will stop you. It might start with a niggling feeling that you need to address some aspect of your life or you may have bigger struggles. If you feel a bit overwhelmed or afraid, that's okay. Doing this exercise might just be the impetus you need to get started. As you are reading this, the likelihood is you are searching for something. You are ready. If you scored:

0-33

It is unlikely that you are spending any time on your personal development and care. You may be feeling very frustrated with life and believe you have little control over what happens. You might have a sense that there has to be more to your existence but you don't know what to do. You don't have a clear sense of purpose or direction. You might feel like you are on a treadmill trying to keep everything going without any joy or sense of fulfillment. You have reached the point where you know that life cannot continue as is. You are ready to try something different and are willing to put in the work.

34-67

Okay. You are self-aware in certain aspects of your life. You have made some changes and you might be doing well in some areas. However, you may lack consistency and still try to control life when things don't go your way. Take a look at where you scored the lowest. Identify small steps you can start to take every day to make improvements. What would a 10 look like? Maybe you are tinkering around the surface of your life and need to dig a bit deeper. There might be some long-standing habits or issues that need addressing. Regardless, you are on the right track. Stick with it.

68-100

Good for you. It looks like you have a good handle on your life and are committed to a path of growth and expansion. You value yourself and realize that a fulfilling life doesn't happen by accident. If you didn't score very highly on the inner space section, I would encourage you to take more silent time out for yourself. It could be just what you need to thrive even more. It will also have a knock-on effect in terms of your overall sense of well-being. Wherever you decide to put your attention, there is always room for improvement. Do you need to refocus? Do you need to surrender more? Maybe revisit your dreams and your vision for your life.

Taking action

Be your own Guru. Whatever your score, I encourage you to start living from the *InsideOut*. I suggest that you pick one or two areas to start with. Decide on a few practices that you are going to implement and commit to making space for them in your day. It doesn't matter how small they may seem, it all makes a difference. This is about valuing yourself and developing healthy habits that will support you through the ups and downs of life. You will start to feel a momentum take hold and there will be no going back. I have listed a few suggestions and tips on the following pages. Many are practices that I follow or have learnt from others. You can pick and choose what works for you and also search out other activities that resonate. Developing your own personalized daily practice is one of the most life-affirming things you can do for yourself.

Inner Space

- For me this is number one. This place of stillness is the source of everything in my life. However skeptical you might be, if life isn't working out for you the way you hoped, it might just be the motivation you need to try something different. Life was definitely not working out the way that I had hoped and I had reached the end of the line. You could start as I did, by doing some research, reading books or going online. When I first started to feel this desire to go deeper into life, I spent all my free time searching out books, mentors and teachers – anything that would help me understand what I was experiencing. They kept showing up. They still do. This is how I spent most of my time while recovering from cancer. The path of seeker is now my path in life. If you do nothing else for now, put your focus here. The effects will gradually ripple out into the world in unimaginable ways and you really will start to trust life.

- Start a meditation practice. You could begin with five minutes a day and gradually build up to whatever time feels right for you. It might be ten minutes, twenty or even half an hour. Consistency is key. If you prefer silence, you can just sit in a quiet location where you won't be disturbed and follow your breath in and out. You might prefer to follow a guided meditation or visualization. That is perfectly fine too. There are many online resources available. The Chopra Center (www.chopra.com) offers many different 21-day practices, and regularly offers them for free. YouTube also has plenty to choose from or you can download one of the many meditation apps available. You might start with the single objective of quieting your busy ego mind, but with time you may find yourself merging into an ocean of stillness. That's the true prize.

- Take up a yoga, Tai Chi or Qi gong class. They are proven ways of lowering your stress levels. I attended a Tai Chi class in Cancer Care West while recovering from treatment and it really calmed my system, especially when I started to feel anxious about my future. I found a yoga nidra class and that too was really relaxing. Practicing present moment awareness switches on that all important parasympathetic nervous system and brings us to a place of internal quiet.

- Get outdoors into nature. I really felt the benefits when I started taking long, daily walks during lockdown. Slowing down in this way brought me deeper into life and the moment. If I miss a day, I really feel the difference. Nature soothes and calms me. I had never realized how disconnected I had become from the natural world and how much I missed it. Not only do I feel recharged afterwards, some of my best ideas and insights come from this quiet time out.

Intuition

- It is much easier to hear this gentle voice when your mind is quiet. That is why meditation is so helpful for tuning into your intuition. Try to be open and trusting, otherwise you will find it very difficult. *A Course in Miracles* says – *Infinite patience produces immediate results.* This is a loving voice that only wants the best for you. Cultivate a relationship with this voice and you will have a cheerleader on board that always has your highest interests at heart.
- Start by doing an experiment for even one day. Decide that you are going to follow any intuitive urges or strong feelings you get. It is important not to confuse them with more ego-based thoughts that arise. This is a different voice. Intuitive thoughts and feelings are gentle, usually free of emotion and they are there to guide you. It can take practice to distinguish between your intuition and fear-based thoughts or addictions. For example, if you get the urge to binge on sugary food or to lash out at someone, it is definitely not your intuition at work.
- Pay attention in your daily life. It could be people you meet, words they say that resonate with you, a book you happen upon, a song you hear on the radio. This is not

about over-analyzing every minute detail. It is about being present in your life. When you get used to tuning in like this, you will quickly know what is significant and what isn't. You will soon be able to decipher when you are being guided to do something. You can have fun with it. It might come in the form of hunches, repetitive thoughts or images. It will be different for each of us, so get to know how your intuition communicates with you. While writing this book I was guided every step of the way. From ideas for chapters, research to carry out and experiences to share, I just knew what to do. I didn't have to *work* to figure it out. I did the work. It just wasn't arduous mental work. I developed a daily writing routine and I worked to get down on paper any intuitive guidance or inspiration as it arose. I wanted to stay in the flow and not miss anything. I often used a voice recorder or notebook to capture any ideas when I was out and about. I still do.

- Intuition isn't science. It is something very different, so I would urge you not to overthink or believe that if things don't happen as you hoped that it's not working. With awareness and practice it can start to be a really helpful force in your life. First we have to trust and let go of the need to be in control. We may not like what it is nudging us to do, but it only wants the best for us. It could be encouraging us to heal or process some painful aspect of our lives so that we can move on. As difficult as that might seem, it is a lot more difficult to shove our feelings down. We just continue to suffer every day.

- Ask for guidance or a sign. Put it out to the universe and let it go. Then just pay attention in the coming hours, days or weeks. Remember, there is a divine timing in our lives and results come in many forms. My experience is that I am given the next step, not the entire road ahead, so belief and trust is essential. I experience guidance as a sense of deep knowing and resonance in my body. I just know when to take action.

- It can be hard to let go in this way initially. This isn't a way of *forcing* life to give you what you want. It is about *letting* life show you what is next on your journey of growth and evolution. You have free will so you can always ignore the voice if it doesn't feel right or if you decide that you are not ready yet. The voice won't abandon you though. It will keep nudging you until you are ready to listen.

Creativity

- First things first. Don't dismiss the idea that creativity is an integral part of your life. Living creatively is not just for those pursuing a career in the creative arts. It is why we are all here. We are the products of creative energy and we are meant to find our unique form of self-expression on earth. If we deny this aspect of ourselves completely, we are headed for illness or depression or some other downfall. I definitely was. Creative expression is an intrinsic part of a healthy, fulfilling life.

- If you don't have a creative outlet right now, think back to when you were a child or teenager. What did you enjoy doing that was free of structure? What soothed you? Is there something that you gave up because you thought it too frivolous as an adult?

- Search out an activity that you have never tried. Pick something that interests you. Try it just for the sheer joy of doing it. I found my way back to knitting after cancer. I had forgotten how much I loved it as a teenager. One thing leads to another. Once you uncork your creativity, like water, it will flow into your life in the most unexpected ways.

- Check out *The Artist's Way* book by Julia Cameron. It is for everyone and it will help you understand how vitally important creativity is. It is not something separate from you that you *do*. It is *you* brought to life through some form of expression in the world. Exercises like the Morning Pages or journaling are great ways to uncover what is going on inside. They can help you get unstuck or find inspiration.

- Give yourself permission to daydream. Sit and do nothing. Have no distractions. See where your attention wanders. Notice any ideas or nudges that just appear out of thin air. These are the seeds of your creativity bursting through. My ideas for writing always pop up when I'm driving, out walking or just sitting looking out the window. It is in the quiet, the nothingness, that creative sparks emerge. They are subtle and fast-moving, so we must be quiet and available. Have a pen and paper handy to capture them. Avoid analysis and don't dismiss anything. Go with the flow and see where it leads.

Beliefs

- Start to observe your thought patterns on a typical day. Just notice what your self-talk sounds like. Is it positive or negative? Michael Singer talks about the *inner roommate* in our head that never stops commenting on everything, usually negatively. As he points out, if the voice were a person, you wouldn't spend much time with them. Commit to separating yourself from this voice and changing your relationship with it.

- When you notice a negative thought, take a breath and say an affirmation. This disrupts the momentum before you go down the rabbit hole. Some examples are: *I hand this worry over* or *This too shall pass.* Find affirmations that ring true for you.

- Don't fight with your thoughts. What we resist persists. Thoughts naturally bubble up and disappear unless we engage with them. Remember that you are not your thoughts. Start a practice of observing them. If you get entangled, a story will unfold and you will live through that reality in your mind with all the associated emotions. I still do this, but less often than I used to, because I have become conscious of what is happening. It is a constant practice to let go before it is too late. Remember the prize is peace. Every teacher I have learnt from says the same thing. Keep letting go. And when you think you have let go, let go some more. That is the practice.

- I found it very helpful to learn that we all have old programs running inside, outdated paradigms and ways of being that no longer serve us. We inherit many of these from family, our culture and society, but it doesn't mean that they have to hold true for us. It was great news to learn that I was entitled to my own belief systems and didn't have to automatically adopt the beliefs of those around me. Become aware of the belief systems you are playing in and buying into. Do they reflect who you are? Do they add value to your life? If not, let them go. There are as many belief systems as there are people. Your beliefs are a key item in your toolbox for living. Make sure the ones that you adopt resonate with you and are supportive.

Appreciation

- When you start to cultivate an attitude of gratitude, you will find yourself smiling more throughout the day. Start by focusing on all that is good in your life. We all have much to be grateful for. Feel into it. Opening your heart in this way really shifts your energy. Do what it takes to feel grateful. On a challenging day, keep it simple. It could be a smile from a stranger, a thank you or a nice meal. Some days it might be all you can do to refrain from complaining. That's fine too.

- Start a gratitude journal. Commit to writing down three or more things that you are grateful for every day. Keeping a journal is a good resource when you are struggling. You can return to the wealth of abundance in it when life feels challenging. If that feels like too much work, just focus on what you are grateful for as you lie in bed or are going about your day. Keep in mind that whatever you give your energy to expands. Over time it does make a difference.

- As a test, write down a list of everything you are appreciative of. How do you feel? Now write a second list of all the things you are dissatisfied with. I didn't have a problem making the second list a long list when I first started. How do you feel now? How do you want to feel? You must shift your focus if you want to start feeling good more of the time. It is that simple.

- I now view life as happening *for* me not *to* me. That wasn't always the case. It doesn't mean I don't struggle or feel down. It is just that now I have a way out. I let myself feel and go through what I need to go through. I try not to stuff down or bypass uncomfortable feelings. By now I know that they always resurface. This was the case with my marriage breakdown and with cancer. They were trying to help me heal some aspect of my life. It might sound an odd thing to say, but I know they happened *for* me and I am very grateful to them now. I had to experience the darkness so that I could really appreciate the light, and I do.

Boundaries

- Holding healthy boundaries is a sign that you are taking personal responsibility for your life. Boundaries are the linchpin of living well and without them you will just end up being battered by whatever comes your way. Supporting others should never be at the expense of your own well-being, so pay attention if you feel you are being called to give more than feels comfortable for you. Being clear on your boundaries is asserting your right to be healthy and well. Know that others will naturally try to push past your boundaries. It's not personal. It is just human nature as we all seek to have our own needs met.

- You must know your values to know your boundaries. Say a value of yours is having an optimistic and constructive attitude to life, but you still spend time in the company of people who complain and are negative. There is no boundary there. As well as knowing your boundaries, you need to know the action you will take to support them. In this case you either don't join in the negative talk or you just politely excuse yourself and leave. Boundaries are about you (not anyone else) and you are entitled to do what is right for you and keeps you healthy. Setting boundaries becomes automatic with practice and will greatly boost your sense of self.

- Take time to consider the relationships in your life, particularly those that you find stressful. If you are feeling distressed or upset by them, it is a sure sign that a boundary has been crossed. What is okay in terms of how someone speaks to you or what they ask of you? What do you need from them? Completing the following sentences will help you get clear:

  People may not......

  I have a right to ask for......

To protect my time and energy it's okay to......

- Observe others who have healthy boundaries and learn from them. It is possible to maintain healthy boundaries in a way that is both loving and firm. I know many people who do. You will feel better about yourself and people will respect you more as a result.

Emotional Ease

- Emotions continually move through us. They are simply energy that bubbles up in response to the meaning we assign to a moment and they need to be released. They can be the result of our thoughts or triggered by some outside event or interaction. If we don't feel them at the time, they lodge in our system and stagnate. We are only postponing the inevitable. Find a safe place, sit quietly and let them move through you. Although it may feel strange initially, once you practice this you will start to clear the residue and feel much lighter. With time you really will move through the ups and downs of life more easily. I guarantee you that.

- If you need help letting go of old hurts that are buried deep and holding you back, commit to talking to someone. A good way to recognize if you have some work to do is to pay attention when you are triggered by things that people say or do. If I feel an emotional charge in a situation, I know that I need to address something within myself. It is *never* about the other person. Confide in a good friend or find a counselor you feel comfortable talking to. Do a bit of research and make sure the person is a good fit before you make a commitment. It is important that you feel understood and safe. When you have dealt with your own *inner thorns,* in the words of Michael A. Singer, you will be unaffected by the emotional prods or behaviors of others. They will roll off you because you have no interest. They have nothing to stick to. There is no wound there to aggravate.

- There are lots of activities that help release emotions. Some that I have practiced are breath work, art therapy, journaling and movement. I attended a workshop based on the late Gabrielle Roth's 5Rhythms' free-form dance and loved it. The 5Rhythms website describes the practice: *a dynamic way to both workout and to meditate in the same breath. They teach us that life is energy in motion, freeing us from any fixed notions about people, places, objects or ideas.*

- Physical therapies like massage or reflexology also have their place. Often when we're very stuck, creating movement and flow in the body can trigger our emotions to release. From my experience it is not enough to just talk about how we feel. Talking is extremely important. It helps us process what is happening, but it does not necessarily release the energy. It must be released physically and safely. Otherwise it can erupt in angry exchanges or overreactions to outside events. In the longer term, unprocessed emotions leave us feeling depressed and sick. Working with an energy healer or craniosacral therapist is another way to deal with them. Trust what feels right for you.

Values

- I look on my values as my personal code of conduct. They are qualities that are particularly important to me. What comes to mind straight away when you think of your values? In my case, I discovered a value of kindness. I try to be kind because I feel a lot better when I am, and I believe it is who I am at my core. As a result, I steer clear of negative people or gossip. I definitely don't read or watch news or social media commentary that is full of anger and vitriol. I believe in a world where we are free to be ourselves. We are sovereign beings, each with our own voice, values, truths and unique purpose. Honoring this is number one for me.

- Do you know what your values are? What are the core things that are non-negotiable in your life? If you don't know, start by writing a list of all the qualities that you hold dear – honesty, connection, integrity, fun, adventure etc. Write down as many as you can. Think about your work or what makes you happy. What does this value give you? You want to end up with a list of three or four core values. This brings a focus to your decision-making and can actually make it easier. You can rule out choices that will compromise them. We suffer when we compromise our values repeatedly.

- To help prompt you, consult lists of core values. There are plenty available online. Ideally, you uncover them by looking at your life. Here are some questions to help reveal them:

  – Think of a meaningful (peak) moment in your life. What were you doing? Who were you with? What value were you honoring?

  – Consider a difficult (peak) moment, when you were angry or upset. What was going on? How were you feeling? Who were you with?
  What value were you suppressing?

  – What is most important in your life, once your basic needs are met? What else do you need to feel fulfilled and at peace? Creative outlets, adventure, learning, silence, etc.

- To what degree are you living your values? Are they just words on a piece of paper or do your behaviors reflect them? If you are feeling frustrated in life, it is likely you are dishonoring some aspect of yourself. You need to know what your values are first before you can do anything about it.

Purpose

- Don't chase success, follow your joy. This wise advice has stayed with me. It is how we tune in and find our purpose. Follow the path of your natural desires, talents and passions with the intention of bringing joy to yourself and others. That is the purpose of life – to be of service in a way that benefits you and others. I learnt this from Wayne Dyer. If you want to find meaning in your life, find a way to be of service. I got it backwards for a long time. I tried to find a destination, or a career, not realizing that who I am showing up as every day is my purpose. It is right here and now. Don't miss out on the clues that life is giving you. Follow the breadcrumb trail of what makes you feel alive. You will then automatically know the next right step. Keep this at the back of your mind no matter what you are doing.

- Spend some time reflecting and writing about this. It isn't necessarily about finding one big goal that you will work towards, but more about how you go about your daily life, how you bring your purpose to life all of the time. It is not something you switch on and off. Maybe it is that you are a really good listener, you make people laugh, you relax people or you are warm. Your very presence is a purpose in itself.

- Reflect on difficult periods in your life and what you learnt from them. There are clues to your purpose in your life story and sometimes you need to spend time unpacking it. You have unique pearls of wisdom to offer even if you don't believe it at this point in time. Tune in and really get a sense of what the story of your life is telling you so far. You might be surprised at what you have learnt and how you can be of service to others. Your true purpose is always linked to being of service. Whatever you have been through, there is always someone on the path right behind you. They are going through a similar experience right now, and when they're ready, you can help them in more ways than you might think.

Self-Care

- Commit to one small act of self-care every day. It doesn't matter how insignificant it may seem, it builds up over time. Prioritizing your needs is an important signal to yourself and those around you that you matter. Your actions teach others to look after themselves too. We learn, not from what people tell *us* to do but by what *they* do. Actions do indeed speak louder than words.

- Say *No* to one thing you don't want to do. It will give you time to focus on what you really want to do. The world will not fall apart if you prioritize your needs. In fact, others will benefit as we are all affected by the moods and energy of others. Consciously spreading good vibes has a bigger impact than we know.

- If you find it hard to put some time aside to look after yourself, I would really encourage you to consider why. Even if it's when you wake up or just before going to sleep, something as simple as taking three slow, deep breaths might be a start. Did you find time for self-care when we were all forced to isolate during COVID-19? If you didn't, then time may not be your problem. Take a look at what is really going on. You cannot change anything until you face up to the truth of it. Change is not always easy, so working with a professional might be the solution if you find it especially difficult.

- If you start to feel overwhelmed during the day, do things that ground and center you. Get into your body. By that I mean, be fully here. You can do this in many ways. You can stand/walk outdoors in your bare feet. You can ground yourself by focusing on your breath. Count the duration of your in-breath e.g. seven seconds and then moderate the out-breath so they are balanced. At the end of each in- and out-breath, hold your breath for a few seconds. Make sure your shoulders are relaxed. You will be surprised how a short practice like this can disrupt any agitation or stress, at least temporarily. Sometimes if I'm out and about and I feel a bit ungrounded or my energy is a bit unsettled, I just set the intention to ground and I can feel it happen.

- Nurture your soul. Set time aside to settle into the innate rhythm of life and listen to your innermost calling. This is the highest form of self-care in my book. Body, mind and spirit align. Everything relaxes and flows. You start to work with life rather than succumbing to the demands of the ego. You move with life rather than resisting and suffering. We all know that the ego is never satisfied. It does everything it can to keep you fighting with life so that it can hold on to the illusion of control. Don't let victim consciousness keep you small. Now more than ever it is essential to engage with the most important person in your life – you.

As I move into a new stage of my life, I am very grateful for all the experiences I have had. Tough as they were at the time, I know every single one of them happened for me. What could have been just a brief interlude with illness has opened me up to a whole new world. Choosing a path of growth and evolution can be challenging at times, but it has a great prize – personal freedom. We free ourselves from the ego. We let go of limiting beliefs and fear. We expose any unconscious programming that holds us back and heal old wounds that keep us stuck. We come face to face with who we really are. That's the miracle. The sky's the limit after that. That is my wish for you.

I can say for sure that no amount of studying and reading could have brought me to where I am now. They have helped me enormously, yet I am different because of cancer. I am different because of everything I have lived through. I am different because of my life experiences. The greatest wisdom and insight comes from living deeply, facing a crisis and seeing it as an opportunity to wake up to the truth of who you are. The impact is far beyond any intellectual knowledge. It is an opportunity to get to know who you really are, a powerful and sovereign, creator being. There is no going back after that. So ironically, a year out of my life, as the consultant said, turned into the year that I learnt how to live. Remember,

You've always had the power, my dear. You just had to learn it for yourself.
The Wizard of Oz

Returning to the words of John O'Donohue, in time I did come to understand what my illness came to tell me and what it wanted me to know. I have embarked on my own new beginning and that has been the greatest gift of all. I will finish as I started, with his timeless wisdom. Every time I read his work, I feel like the words were written specifically for me, and they were. His words speak from a place deep within us all. When we connect with that place, we meet each other. I look forward to meeting you.

Though your destination is not yet clear
You can trust the promise of this opening;
Unfurl yourself into the grace of beginning
That is at one with your life's desire.
Awaken your spirit to adventure;
Hold nothing back, learn to find ease in risk;
Soon you will be home in a new rhythm,
For your soul senses the world that awaits you.
Extract – For a New Beginning
by John O'Donohue

Author Biography

Celine O'Donovan is a native of Galway city on the west coast of Ireland. Following a successful, international career in marketing, she is now a published author.

This change in direction was accelerated by personal lessons Celine learnt after her diagnosis with breast cancer and its aftermath.

Her message: nothing happens by chance and all life events are sent to spur spiritual growth and enable us fulfill our individual gifts.

This reframing of how we see our lives now shapes Celine's writing. Her mission is to create personal and practical "epiphany" moments that allow her readers to discover this for themselves.

Previous Title

The Tapestry of Life
A work of fiction, this book is a tribute to the powerful community of people that helped Celine on the road to recovery.
The story is set in Galway city, Ireland, and follows three generations of women as they try to find their place in the world. Over the course of a few weeks, their lives collide and they are changed forever as a result. Themes of community, belonging and friendship are at the heart of this warm-hearted story.
Publisher – Tribes Press
Date – October 2019
ISBN: 978-1-9124411-13-6

Note To Reader

Thank you for purchasing *Gifts from the Devastation*. I really hope that you enjoyed reading it as much as I did writing it. If you have a few moments, please feel free to add your review of the book at your favorite online site for feedback. Also, if you would like to find out more about me, read my blog posts or connect with me directly, please visit my website: www.celineodonovan.com

Sincerely, Celine

References

Epigraph
Mary Oliver (1963) "The Journey"

Preface
John O'Donohue (2007) "A Blessing for a Friend on the Arrival of Illness," *Benedictus: A Book of Blessings*. UK: Bantam Press

Introduction
Ram Dass, www.beherenownetwork.com

Chapter 1
Mary Oliver (1992) "The Summer Day"
Carmel Conway, Spirit Healing Angel Shop, www.facebook.com/spirithealingangelshop

Chapter 2
Abraham Hicks, www.quotespedia.org

Chapter 3
Wayne Dyer, www.entrepreneur.com
Brandon Bays (2002) *The Journey*. US: Simon and Schuster
Anita Moorjani (2012) *Dying to Be Me*. UK: Hay House

Chapter 4
Allanah Hunt, www.allanahhunt.com
Dr. Yvonne Murphy, www.divineclearing.com

Chapter 5
Kahlil Gibran (1923) "On Pain," *The Prophet*. US: Knopf

Chapter 6
Clare Dakin, www.treesisters.org

Chapter 7

Rumi, www.themindsjournal.com

Mooji, www.mooji.tv

Chapter 8

Anita Moorjani (2012) *Dying to Be Me*. UK: Hay House

Chapter 9

Oprah Winfrey, www.goalcast.com

Cancer Care West, www.cancercarewest.ie

Dr. Yvonne Murphy, www.divineclearing.com

Dr. Dilis Clare, www.drclareapothecary.com

Una Mc Nerney, Anois Holistic Therapies, www.facebook.com/
Anoisholistictherapies

Julia Cameron (1994) *The Artist's Way*. UK: Souvenir Press Ltd.

Margie Connolly, www.margieconnolly.ie

Chapter 10

Jon Kabat-Zinn (1990) *Full Catastrophe Living*. US: Delacorte
Press

Albert Einstein, www.quotefancy.com

Arianna Huffington (2014) *Thrive*. US: Harmony Books

Simon Sinek, www.goalcast.com

Caroline Myss (1996) *Anatomy of the Spirit*. US: Three Rivers
Press

Chapter 11

Heidi DuPree (2015) *Awaken Your Greater Health: How Energy
Medicine Opens the Way to Healing*. US: CreateSpace
Independent Publishing Platform

Victoria Labalme, www.victorialabalme.com/tedx-talk-risk-
forward

Wayne Dyer, "Getting in the Gap Meditation," www.youtube.
com/watch?v=KADc4U2rng0

Chapter 12

Friedrich Koenig, www.goodreads.com

Kahlil Gibran (1923) "On Pain," *The Prophet*. US: Knopf

Lao Tzu (1993) *The Tao Te Ching*. Hackett Publishing

Michael A. Singer (2015) *The Surrender Experiment*. US: Harmony Books

Chapter 13

Abraham Maslow, www.quotefancy.com

Pema Chödrön (2002) *The Places That Scare You: A Guide to Fearlessness in Difficult Times*. US: Shambhala

Michael A. Singer (2007) *The Untethered Soul*. US: New Harbinger Publications

Peter A. Levine, www.somaticexperiencing.com

Mooji (2016) *Vaster Than Sky, Greater Than Space*. US: Sounds True

Chapter 14

Wayne Dyer, www.goodreads.com

Wayne Dyer (2001) *You'll See It When You Believe It*. William Morrow Paperbacks

Marianne Williamson (1992) *A Return to Love: Reflections on the Principles of A Course in Miracles*. US: HarperCollins

Brené Brown, www.brenebrown.com

Rhonda Byrne (2006) *The Secret*. UK: Simon and Schuster

Dr. Joe Dispenza: *Evolve Your Brain* (US: HCI Books, 2007); *Breaking the Habit of Being Yourself* (US: Hay House Inc., 2012); *You are the Placebo* (US: Hay House Inc., 2014); *Becoming Supernatural: How Common People Are Doing the Uncommon* (US: Hay House Inc., 2017)

Dr. Bruce Lipton (2015) *The Biology of Belief*. UK: Hay House UK Ltd.

Centers for Disease Control and Prevention, https://articles. mercola.com/sites/articles/archive/2010/02/04/stress-linked-

to-cancer.aspx
Dr. Candace Pert, www.healingcancer.info/ebook/candace-pert

Chapter 15
Brené Brown, Magic Lessons with Elizabeth Gilbert podcast, Episode 12
Margie Connolly, www.margieconnolly.ie
Julia Cameron (1994) *The Artist's Way*. UK: Souvenir Press Ltd.
Anita Moorjani (2012) *Dying to Be Me*. UK: Hay House
Wayne Dyer, www.drwaynedyer.com
The Dalai Lama, *The Best Quotes Book: 555 Daily Inspirational and Motivational Quotes by Famous People* by Joseph Goodman (2018, www.lulu.com)
Kahlil Gibran (1923) "On Children," *The Prophet*. US: Knopf
J. Sterling Livingston (1988) "Pygmalion in Management." *Harvard Business Review*
Eckhart Tolle (August 9, 2019 – Twitter post)

Chapter 16
Rumi. *Rooh-E-Rumi: Seeking God is Seeking Love* by Mamta Sehgal. India: Notion Press, 2019
Abraham Maslow, Hierarchy of Needs, www.simplypsychology.org/maslow.html
Michael A. Singer (2007) *The Untethered Soul*. US: New Harbinger Publications
Jon Kabat-Zinn (1990) *Full Catastrophe Living*. UK: Bantam Press

Chapter 17
Rumi, www.azquotes.com
Noreen Kiely, kielynoreen@gmail.com
Wayne Dyer (2014) *I Can See Clearly Now*. US: Hay House Inc.
Albert Einstein, www.quora.com
Paulo Coelho (2000) *The Fifth Mountain*. US: HarperOne

Chapter 18
Carl Jung, www.goodreads.com
Viktor Frankl (2004) *Man's Search for Meaning*. UK: Rider, imprint of Ebury Publishing. First published in German in 1946 under the title: *Ein Psycholog erlebt das Konzentrationslager*.
Albert Einstein, www.brainyquote.com

Chapter 19
George Eliot, www.goodreads.com
Anita Moorjani, www.youtube.com/watch?v=iokctou6NhI
Pat Divilly, www.patdivilly.com

Chapter 20
Wayne Dyer, www.brainyquote.com
Richard Branson (April 29, 2015 – Twitter post)
Oprah Winfrey, www.azquotes.com
Albert Einstein, www.azquotes.com
Amy Schmidt, "Abundance," in memory of Mary Oliver, www.rattle.com/abundance-by-amy-schmidt

Chapter 21
Lalah Delia, www.vibratehigherdaily.com/lalah-delia-copyrighted-published-works-permission
Anita Moorjani, www.anitamoorjani.com

Chapter 22
Wayne Dyer (2013) *The Essential Wayne Dyer Collection*. US: Hay House Inc.
Martin Luther King, www.travishellstrom.com/articles/be-great
Deepak Chopra (1994) *The Seven Spiritual Laws of Success*. US: Amber-Allen Publishing
Michael A. Singer (2007) *The Untethered Soul*. US: New Harbinger Publications

Chapter 23

Zachary Quinto, www.brainyquote.com

Abraham Maslow (2000) *The Maslow Business Reader*. US: John Wiley & Sons

Thom Hartmann (1998) *The Last Hours of Ancient Sunlight*. UK: Hodder and Stoughton

Mooji, www.mooji.tv

Michael A. Singer (2007) *The Untethered Soul*. US: New Harbinger Publications

Oprah Winfrey, 21-Day Meditation Experience, chopracentermeditation.com

Benjamin Ramakrishna (2016) *The Hamster Wheel is Not Motorized*. Germany: Ekabhava Publishing

Richard Bach, www.goodreads.com

Wayne Dyer, www.waynedyer.com

Ram Dass, www.beherenownetwork.com

www.thriveglobal.com

www.heartmath.org/resources/downloads/the-energetic-heart/

www.oxfam.org/en/research/time-care

Chapter 24

Anita Moorjani (October 26, 2013 – Facebook post)

Deepak Chopra, www.quotefancy.com

Deepak Chopra, Daily Breath Podcast

Dr. Helen Schucman (2008) *A Course in Miracles*. US: Foundation for Inner Peace, 3rd edition

Dr. Wayne W. Dyer, Podcast

www.chopra.com

Cancer Care West, www.cancercarewest.ie

Julia Cameron (1994) *The Artist's Way*. UK: Souvenir Press Ltd.

Michael A. Singer (2007) *The Untethered Soul*. US: New Harbinger Publications

www.5rhythms.com

www.scottschwenk.com

The Wizard of Oz (1939)

John O'Donohue (2008) "For a New Beginning," *To Bless the Space Between Us: A Book of Blessings*. US: Convergent Books

SPIRITUALITY

O is a symbol of the world, of oneness and unity; this eye
represents knowledge and insight. We publish titles on general
spirituality and living a spiritual life. We aim to inform and help
you on your own journey in this life.
If you have enjoyed this book, why not tell other readers by
posting a review on your preferred book site?

Recent bestsellers from O-Books are:

Heart of Tantric Sex
Diana Richardson
Revealing Eastern secrets of deep love and intimacy to Western
couples.
Paperback: 978-1-90381-637-0 ebook: 978-1-84694-637-0

Crystal Prescriptions
The A-Z guide to over 1,200 symptoms and their healing crystals
Judy Hall
The first in the popular series of eight books, this handy little
guide is packed as tight as a pill-bottle with crystal remedies for
ailments.
Paperback: 978-1-90504-740-6 ebook: 978-1-84694-629-5

Take Me To Truth
Undoing the Ego
Nouk Sanchez, Tomas Vieira
The best-selling step-by-step book on shedding the Ego, using the
teachings of *A Course In Miracles*.
Paperback: 978-1-84694-050-7 ebook: 978-1-84694-654-7

The 7 Myths about Love...Actually!
The Journey from your HEAD to the HEART of your SOUL
Mike George
Smashes all the myths about LOVE.
Paperback: 978-1-84694-288-4 ebook: 978-1-84694-682-0

The Holy Spirit's Interpretation of the New Testament
A Course in Understanding and Acceptance
Regina Dawn Akers
Following on from the strength of *A Course In Miracles*, NTI
teaches us how to experience the love and oneness of God.
Paperback: 978-1-84694-085-9 ebook: 978-1-78099-083-5

The Message of A Course In Miracles
A translation of the Text in plain language
Elizabeth A. Cronkhite
A translation of *A Course in Miracles* into plain, everyday
language for anyone seeking inner peace. The companion
volume, *Practicing A Course In Miracles*, offers practical lessons
and mentoring.
Paperback: 978-1-84694-319-5 ebook: 978-1-84694-642-4

Your Simple Path
Find Happiness in every step
Ian Tucker
A guide to helping us reconnect with what is really important in our lives.
Paperback: 978-1-78279-349-6 ebook: 978-1-78279-348-9

365 Days of Wisdom
Daily Messages To Inspire You Through The Year
Dadi Janki
Daily messages which cool the mind, warm the heart and guide you along your journey.
Paperback: 978-1-84694-863-3 ebook: 978-1-84694-864-0

Body of Wisdom
Women's Spiritual Power and How it Serves
Hilary Hart
Bringing together the dreams and experiences of women across the world with today's most visionary spiritual teachers.
Paperback: 978-1-78099-696-7 ebook: 978-1-78099-695-0

Dying to Be Free
From Enforced Secrecy to Near Death to True Transformation
Hannah Robinson
After an unexpected accident and near-death experience, Hannah Robinson found herself radically transforming her life, while a remarkable new insight altered her relationship with her father, a practising Catholic priest.
Paperback: 978-1-78535-254-6 ebook: 978-1-78535-255-3

The Ecology of the Soul
A Manual of Peace, Power and Personal Growth for Real People
in the Real World
Aidan Walker
Balance your own inner Ecology of the Soul to regain your
natural state of peace, power and wellbeing.
Paperback: 978-1-78279-850-7 ebook: 978-1-78279-849-1

Not I, Not other than I
The Life and Teachings of Russel Williams
Steve Taylor, Russel Williams
The miraculous life and inspiring teachings of one of the World's
greatest living Sages.
Paperback: 978-1-78279-729-6 ebook: 978-1-78279-728-9

On the Other Side of Love
A woman's unconventional journey towards wisdom
Muriel Maufroy
When life has lost all meaning, what do you do?
Paperback: 978-1-78535-281-2 ebook: 978-1-78535-282-9

Practicing A Course In Miracles
A translation of the Workbook in plain language, with
mentor's notes
Elizabeth A. Cronkhite
The practical second and third volumes of The Plain-Language
A Course In Miracles.
Paperback: 978-1-84694-403-1 ebook: 978-1-78099-072-9

Quantum Bliss
The Quantum Mechanics of Happiness, Abundance, and Health
George S. Mentz
Quantum Bliss is the breakthrough summary of success and spirituality secrets that customers have been waiting for.
Paperback: 978-1-78535-203-4 ebook: 978-1-78535-204-1

The Upside Down Mountain
Mags MacKean
A must-read for anyone weary of chasing success and happiness
– one woman's inspirational journey swapping the uphill slog for the downhill slope.
Paperback: 978-1-78535-171-6 ebook: 978-1-78535-172-3

Your Personal Tuning Fork
The Endocrine System
Deborah Bates
Discover your body's health secret, the endocrine system, and 'twang' your way to sustainable health!
Paperback: 978-1-84694-503-8 ebook: 978-1-78099-697-4

Readers of ebooks can buy or view any of these bestsellers by clicking on the live link in the title. Most titles are published in paperback and as an ebook. Paperbacks are available in traditional bookshops. Both print and ebook formats are available online.
Find more titles and sign up to our readers' newsletter at http://www.johnhuntpublishing.com/mind-body-spirit
Follow us on Facebook at https://www.facebook.com/OBooks/ and Twitter at https://twitter.com/obooks